S0-BYU-453

A Choir Director's Handbook

A Choir Director's Handbook

Compiled and Edited
by

Andrea (Noni) Wells Miller

With Contributions from

Will K. Andress	Neal Knighton
David S. Blackburn	Andrea Wells Miller
Dudley Blakeney	Mack M. Moore
E. Martene Craig	Lloyd Ogilvie
Richard Dinwiddie	John Purifoy
Aubrey Edwards	Sonny Salsbury
Cam Floria	Katy Stokes
Owen Griffin	Pat Terry
Kurt Kaiser	Lee White

John R. Wyatt

WORD
EDUCATIONAL PRODUCTS DIVISION

Word, Inc.
Waco, Texas

A CHOIR DIRECTOR'S HANDBOOK

ISBN 0–8499–8160–3

Contents

About the Editor

Several experiences have combined to give Andrea Wells Miller the qualifications and opportunity to produce *The Choir Director's Handbook.* A Bachelor of Arts in Music degree (Furman University) provided the *formal knowledge* of music and musicians. Nine years with Word Incorporated's music publishing division provided the *practical experience.*

At Word, working with composers from around the world provided *insight* into the intentions of each composer and the potential impact of their music.

Contact with thousands of ministers of music in a series of national workshops provided *awareness* of areas of music ministry for which the choir director receives no formal training (i.e. music schools, seminaries).

Close communication with persons who had explored these practical areas of need provided *resources* from which to draw helpful information.

Coordinating a complex network of marketing programs and promotion campaigns sharpened the *organizational skills* needed to pull eighteen authors' experiences together.

The merging of these qualifications and opportunities produced *The Choir Director's Handbook.* We are confident it will provide the inspiration and information needed to help you add exciting new dimensions to your music ministry.

The Publishers

How to Use This Handbook

SPECIFIC NEED: A glance at the table of contents tells you that there are many areas of choral music ministry addressed in these pages. There may be one specific area you've been thinking about starting. Concentrating on one special area is one of the most efficient ways to get something going. One way to use this book is to turn to that specific area and start working on it.

OVERALL SCOPE: Sometimes, even when things seem to be going extremely well, a sense of restlessness or boredom sets in. This could be a sign that you're ready to grow, but you're not quite sure where to start. Reading these articles through might give you a place to begin—that one area that really excites you as you read. One way to use this book is to read it all, searching for a new way to grow and put challenge and freshness into your church music ministry.

BUILDING PLAN: Perhaps there is more than one area you would like to begin. One way to use this book is to first plan a strategy for beginning and then add each new area you select. Keep the handbook nearby for reference as each new area comes into your plans.

Preface

I hung up the phone and let out a deep breath as I reached for my dictaphone. "Memo to Kurt Kaiser and John Purifoy," I began, and then clicked off the recorder to think. The man to whom I had spoken on the phone was a minister of music who wanted to talk to someone about his specific church situation.

"The people here have talent, are willing to work, and they seem to be open to trying new things," he had said. "But where can we go to find out how to do some of the new and exciting things we see happening in other churches? How do those people do it?"

He had started doing what I often do when I'm at the end of my own knowledge—asking around. One of the sources he had chosen was a music publisher, so he had called Word. Since I was then in the marketing division, I spent a few minutes with him talking about his situation. I told him about things I had heard other choir directors say they had done, and the man had a few new ideas while we talked. But I still wanted to pass on this need for information to others in the music division of our company.

Trying to focus these thoughts into a paragraph for my dictaphone was difficult, and I finally gave up and filed the phone call away in the back of my mind with the others like it that happened every week, and went on with the work at hand.

A few weeks later at an annual Christian Booksellers' Convention, the subject came up again while I was standing in the company booth with a few sales representatives. This time it came from the book and music store personnel themselves. A salesman asked me if I knew of a book which would answer some of the questions that choir directors kept asking the clerks in the stores. None of us knew of such a book, but once again I thought of that choir director asking around—this time in a music store. I started thinking about what it would be like if there were places where choir directors could go to get some answers. And then it occurred to me that perhaps the best way to find out about how to do some of these things would be to ask people who are really doing them. Two of the sales representatives, Grady Baskin and Denny Bray, also thought this approach would be of help. So I wrote to some of the men and women I had met who have developed ways to do one or another of these areas. I asked them to write about how they do what they do and how they have gone about developing their ideas. The result of their writing is this collection.

In the process of watching these articles unfold, I was amazed at what I learned! And since none of the authors had any idea what the others would say on the different subjects, any repeated ideas seem only to confirm that there may be some common principles which serve as a basis for developing a more creative, relevant and healthy ministry through music.

At this point I would like to say a special "thanks" to each author. All of them gave unselfishly of their knowledge and experience, and were willing to be open about the "behind the scenes" part of doing these various areas. Also I wish to thank Ken Barker, Jim Broaddus, Keith Miller and Russ O'Dell for their reading of the manuscript and helpful suggestions.

It is my hope that this collection will help meet the need for more knowledge in some areas of church music ministry. I believe that God communicates—through prayer, through the Bible, through other people, and countless other ways. Perhaps an idea read here, modified or embellished by your own creativity and knowledge of your unique situation, may provide refreshing new energy for your ministry.

ANDREA WELLS MILLER
Waco, Texas

Getting Started

John R. Wyatt

1.

How to Achieve Excitement and Momentum in a Choir Program and Keep It

From the editor: *No matter what career stage you may be in, one of the main concerns that seems to be shared by almost every choir director I know is how to get those talented, busy, sharp people out there in the pews to move up to the choir loft and stay there. And it seems to me that this is a natural place to start this book, for without excitement and momentum, much of the rest of these articles would be hard to apply in a real church situation.*

Here are some practical suggestions from a minister of music who started with a small choir in a church from a town of 28,000 people and led the choir in growth and musical ability until there were over a hundred people in it and even more on the waiting list! How did he do it?

I've studied many successful, effective music ministries. One thing I've noticed. There are always many excited, motivated people. I've asked myself, "What's basic? What principles are being applied that I can discover and apply myself? How can I stir up excitement in my own choir program? How can I achieve momentum?" (By momentum I mean that I don't feel like I'm the only one who cares. A choir full of excited people have come to share my dream and will pay the price to see it come true.)

I've studied others and I've experimented on my own. I believe

I've distilled some answers from what I've learned and I am excited to share them.

The age group could be children, teenagers, college or adult. The size may be small or large. The congregation might be conservative or progressive, formal or informal. The stylistic norm might tend toward gospel or the classics.

All sorts of individuals succeed in achieving excitement and momentum. I've seen it. The minister of music may be well organized or he may "fly by the seat of his pants." He may be an accomplished musician or he may be somewhat limited. He may possess a wonderful personality and then again, he may not. He may not even be a "he." He may be one of the many wonderful female ministers of music.

The only times I've had trouble making these principles work were when I was either fearful or lazy. I am tempted often to be both, but our God is a God of courage and strength. Each of us can draw on him. So take courage. Take strength. Be bold and work hard. Build a choir program that will attract the sharpest people in your town. Build choirs that can make God's praise glorious.

The principles I refer to can be boiled down to a basic formula:

HIGH REWARD + HIGH REQUIREMENT = MOMENTUM

I have often been angry and discouraged when people who "ought" to be in the choir weren't or when people who were in choir weren't as faithful as they "ought" to be. I've preached sermons to the people who were present concerning those who were not. I have even fired some hot letters into the mail so that everyone would get the benefit of my motivational gems. But the results of such steaming about have been terribly unsatisfactory. People are not motivated by "ought to's." They never have been, and it is not likely that they ever will be.

High Reward

My dad raised cattle when I was a boy. I saw him work for hours trying to drive a dozen old heifers and a couple of bulls through a gate in the fence row. He would get one in and two would get out. It was enough to drive a Baptist preacher up the wall. But then I remember other times when he would just walk out there and raise his voice in a familiar call. The cattle would look up and see the bucket of feed in his hand and come through that same gate with no trouble at all. My choir members have, of course, little in common with my dad's old heifers and bulls. But there is one thing. They come when there is food in the trough.

It is much easier to draw people through the gate of faithful involvement than to drive them through it. A "want to" works better than an "ought to" almost every time.

When it is *rewarding,* they come flocking. I just keep working on my plan each year until I am convinced that it is going to be rewarding to be a member of the choir. Here are three questions I ask myself to determine if the plan is ready:

1. Is what I've planned going to be interesting? I've seen people spend much money, travel many miles, and allocate huge amounts of time in search of something interesting. People are hungry to be interested. The feeling of interest surging up in one's being is rewarding. If I can fill this need, I can fill my choir loft.

2. Is there ample opportunity for individual growth? It's rewarding to accomplish something personally. Growth, improvement, and achievement are rewarding. One may say, "I don't think I can do it." I show them how. I encourage them. I believe in them. I give them a chance. They do it! They are thrilled. If such possibilities are part of the plan, I believe I have a winner.

3. Is what I've planned going to be challenging to the group as a whole? It is rewarding to be a part of something bigger than you are. It is rewarding to be a part of a group that accomplishes something. When I can get a group of people pulling together on the same side of a struggle, then I have an excited bunch of people. I keep encouraging. I keep leading the way up the mountain until what seemed impossible has become reality. The view from the top of the mountain is breath-taking. To say the least, it is rewarding. People are hugging each other and jumping up and down and shouting, "We did it!"

Before I can rest about the year's plan, I have to have an enthusiastic "yes" to each of these three questions. It is not always easy. It takes a great deal of prayer, lots of writing and re-writing. But I can't let myself stop until I am there. To get these three "yeses" I have to master two major elements.

1. The routine week-in, week-out work.
2. The occasional climactic event.

Each is essential if the program is to be rewarding. Another equation says it:

HIGH REWARD = QUALITY ROUTINE + CLIMACTIC EVENT

Quality routine could be defined or described in many ways. Here are some things I try to keep in mind.

1. *Quality routine* is the fruit of a leader who goes all out to stay fresh. I try to do my week-in, week-out routine as though everything depended on it every week. I want things happening every week that are fresh and unpredictable. I resist the temptation to "just do" the anthem or hymn arrangement. I try to do something *with* it.

One thing I use to stir up my creativity is the 4/20 brainstorm technique. I have used this technique in handling many different matters. Here is the way I would use the technique in anthem preparation: About six weeks before an anthem is to be performed, I would do these three procedures at least four mornings out of that week.

(1) Read through the anthem's text two or three times.
(2) Read through the anthem two or three times giving special attention to the musical ideas.
(3) Put a pencil to work jotting down observations about the anthem: ideas regarding its performance and ideas relating to how I could rehearse it. I keep jotting until there are at least twenty different items each day. I put down anything that comes to mind. Occasionally there is something significant. Often the best product my mind can create seems shallow or silly, but I keep jotting. Often out of this will come a very tasty, significant idea or two that will add the zest and freshness which turns routine into *quality routine.*

2. A *quality routine* is challenging, but "do-able." I recall a time my choir was simply not getting the music ready. We had scheduled six anthems in the rehearsal, but we were getting through only three or four. The choir president figured it out before I did. "There is too much difficult music," he said.

I knew he was right, so I replaced some of the hard music with easier music. The next rehearsal was fantastic. We were encouraged. We felt like we were accomplishing something. It was still challenging, but now it was "do-able."

3. *A quality routine* contains the security of familiar music and the stimulation of new music. Here is the anthem scheduling formula I use:

(1) One-third new music and real winners that have not been performed during the last three years

(2) Two-thirds out of the music library that were favorites of two and three years ago
(3) Nothing from last year

I feel free to make selected exceptions when I want to or need to.

4. A *quality routine* contains the spice of variety. I try to run as much of the "style gamut" as I can. It would be easy to program for myself or a select few in the choir or congregation. But this is a trap, I think, and I try to avoid it. The spectrum of taste is wide. The wide spectrum represents real live, hungry people, and I want to see all of them fed. Running the gamut helps me keep it interesting for all my choir members.

5. A *quality routine,* above all, must be interesting. I like what I heard Don Fontana * say once. "Look until you find material that has 'wow' . . . with significance." Don simply won't schedule an anthem that does not have "wow." No two people would define "wow" alike. But all of us should keep looking, keep working, and not quit until our work has our own brand of "wow" about it.

Quality routine is basically giving it all you've got week-in and week-out until you are doing extraordinary things with the ordinary resources at your disposal.

I firmly believe that *quality routine* is as vital to a choir program as the front wheel is to a bike. Without it you won't get very far, very easily. You surely won't have much momentum.

But if *quality routine* is all you have, you still don't go anywhere very fast. *Quality routine* is neat. It is wonderful, but at best routine gets boring. Even when routine is interesting, it stops being interesting. You need the back wheel of the bike to really go places. You need the other essential . . . the occasional *climactic event* to keep the spark of interest going.

I will probably never forget the first youth choir rehearsal at a certain church I served a few years ago. Approximately twenty-five timid teenagers sat before me. I heard one gorgeous soprano voice. I noticed a kid on the front row who sounded like the beginnings of a good bass. The other voices could scarcely be heard.

> Diagnosis: Youth Choir is not a "big deal" in this town . . . or even in this church.

---

* Don G. Fontana is Minister of Music, Garden Grove Community Church, Garden Grove, Ca.

Treatment: The *climactic event.* Make plans big enough to excite the sharpest people in town.

What happened? Within six months that little puddle of timidity had become an ocean of excitement. There were 83 bright singers and a dozen sharp adult sponsors. Over 3,000 people came to see their performance of "Celebrate Life" in the town's civic center. Two years later that choir, now 115 strong, performed the World Premiere of Paul Johnson's "Here Comes the Son" at Word's annual workshop in Waco, Texas.

Following that first rehearsal, I had begun to ask myself and others, "What will it take to excite the sharpest people in town? What kind of things are a 'big deal' to the teenagers in this town?" Here are some answers I came up with and the corresponding action I took.

1. It is a "big deal" here for something to take place on the civic center stage. So I rented the civic center. I began to tell people that we were bringing "Celebrate Life" to town and that we would put it on at the civic center. That was pretty bold for a church choir in that town, and people started to perk up.

2. Professional directors give an event the "big deal" flavor. So I hired a professional director. I got one from out of town. That's even better.

3. Things advertised in the media get attention. So I took out ads announcing enrollment interviews for the production chorus of "Celebrate Life" which was coming to the civic center on March 10. The phone started ringing off the wall. There were numerous people from outside the church who called. That's wonderful, but what is better is what began to happen to our own kids. They started getting excited. A bunch of those "hot dogs" who could care less about youth choir before were now starting to come around. The number at rehearsal was over 50 immediately, and it rose into the 80s.

4. Events attended by dignitaries, now that's a big deal! So I invited everyone from President Johnson on down. I posted their replies, and it was exciting to see how many state and local dignitaries said they would come.

5. Things that require time and effort attract people with drive and ability. So I scheduled backbreaking rehearsal schedules. For weeks, we worked two hours on Saturday and again on Sunday. Then the last couple of weeks we worked every night with some rehearsals lasting as long as six hours. I still never found their limit. They were resilient with excitement.

6. Programs that have multiple performance give people op-

tions. So I scheduled three performances: Saturday night, Sunday afternoon, and Sunday evening. Incidentally, I really believe in multiple performances. There is always a potential audience that can't come at 7:00 Sunday evening. I believe in giving them an option. The choir is benefited, too. They have worked hard and love to have more than one chance to perform what they have prepared. Multiple performances upgrade the project in the minds of the audience and the choir alike. I have used this approach many times and have had great success with it. Always in two performances we have had more than we could have seated in one. One other thing, make the final performance at the strongest time. For us, it is usually Sunday night.

You might wonder . . . "Do you get criticism?" Sure! People scream about the cost and the time it takes. Once, I got tired of the criticism and scaled down the program for a whole year. After a few months, I noticed that two things had happened. (1) No one was complaining and (2) no one was coming. The sharp people were busy doing something else.

Talented, energetic, leader type people are all over the place in any town. Those people are going to be busy, up to their noses, doing something. I have determined that I am going to offer opportunities for service and involvement that are so exciting, so big, so tough, and so challenging that the most talented people in my town will simply ache to be a part of what's happening, even if they can't.

I used to worry about conflicts in schedule. Then I realized I didn't need to do that. If what we're doing is exciting enough, everyone else will have to worry about the conflicts in schedule.

Exciting enough is the key. What is exciting one place won't be in another place. What's exciting is relative to the frame of reference in which you work and in which your people live. One rule of thumb is that it be bigger or better than they expect it to be. Another thing to look for is comments of exclamation. When one of your sharper, more demanding choir members sparkles with excitement and says something like, "Hey, this is sharp!", you are there. If folks are bored, you are not there. But don't get side tracked and bogged down trying to match what other choir directors are doing in bigger, more demanding situations. All you have to do is reach past the top of your own *quality routine.*

One more thing: To really be exciting a project has got to be a struggle. If some people aren't griping about the amount of rehearsal time or the cost, or the difficulty of the project, it simply isn't tough enough. People love a struggle. A little griping about how tough it is is music to my ears. One of the most rewarding things in life is close fellowship with a group of people. And fellowship is more likely to be stirred up among people bound together by a common struggle than any other way I have seen.

What if it is actually too tough? That's possible, I suppose, but not nearly as dangerous as if it is too easy. If you should discover that something is too difficult, it is usually easy to modify and simplify. Whatever you do, however, make it something that's a bit difficult to do.

How often should you plan *climactic events?* At first, plan them more often. When things get rolling, more seldom. The next event should be as far off as possible, but close enough to produce excitement. When *climactic events* come too frequently, a fatigue sets in that is actually counter-productive. Also, following each *climactic event* is an inevitable low. The further off the next big push; the further off the next corresponding low. I try to mix in just enough *climactic events* to keep up the momentum and no more than that.

High Requirements

We have discussed *quality routine* and *climactic event.* That wraps up the essentials to high reward. Now, let's consider *high requirements.* I'm of the conviction that *high requirements* are as essential to momentum as air is to a bicycle's tires.

Without *high requirements,* morale is almost always in grave danger of going flat and momentum is lost. When 50 people have done most of the work and 10 others want to jump on the bandwagon to share in the victory, you are likely to have 50 discouraged people. *High requirements* put an end to "tail-end-jumper-oners." *High requirements* put a stop to the "in-and-outers" and the "sometimes-on—sometimes-offers."

My choir president walked out and nearly resigned the first time I had the courage to set and enforce a *high requirement* for the Adult Choir. We were preparing a magnificent major work . . . a *climactic event,* if you please. The schedule called for a full weekend of workshops to learn the music. Three weeks in advance I announced that unless there were at least 80 percent of the enrollment present at those workshop rehearsals, we would not rehearse. Each one planning to be absent was to notify me so I could cancel any rehearsal for which there would be less than 80 percent. My position is that to rehearse with less than

75–80 percent is almost worse than no rehearsal. We would work our hearts out, and then the next rehearsal we would simply have to do much of it over again. This destroys the morale of the really faithful choir members, especially the better musicians.

The Thursday night of the 80 percent rule rolled around. At 30 minutes into the rehearsal, I stopped to count, and we were short of the 114 people needed by about nine people. I said, "Folks, it is very deceiving. With 105 people here we are sounding great, but there are nearly 40 people not here. We must not continue."

The verbal feedback was sudden and furious. People had made special arrangements to be there. Many were incensed that the rehearsal was being cancelled. I asked them why they had said nothing before. I had announced the plan for three weeks. Someone said, "We didn't think you would really do it." I was just about to give in to the cries of "let's go ahead and rehearse" until I heard that. But I suddenly had new determination to stick to my guns! I knew the rule and I must be tested.

As I said, my choir president walked out. Other faithful members kept up the protests. I told one twenty-year veteran, "I'm doing this for you. You are here all the time. I'm trying to protect you from people who are here about half the time spoiling the work you have faithfully done." He seemed to understand. Someone said, "We can't afford to miss this rehearsal. Performance is two weeks away." I said, "I agree, but we are missing it essentially, anyway, even though it doesn't seem like it, since so many are absent."

What happened next was very interesting! One choir member spoke up and said, "John is our leader, and I think we ought to do what he says." There was applause from what seemed like most of the choir. The majority understood and wanted to see *high standards* held up. I felt better. Things started happening. The group captains and several others organized themselves to call every choir member who was absent without notice. They informed them of what had happened.

According to records, we would have enough people present to rehearse the following night, but the same rule stood. About fifteen minutes into the next night's rehearsal, the cry went up that we had just hit 80 percent. Everyone applauded, and we had a *tremendous rehearsal.*

I noticed a different, positive, happy attitude. It was like the calm after the storm. It was the security you feel when you test your leader and he or she passes the test. From that night on, rehearsal attendance was phenomenal. At one regular Tuesday night rehearsal, we had 130 present out of 150 members. When concert time came, we were ready like never before!

Since that experience, a colleague of mine has taught me another principle that should be observed in making and enforcing rules. (1) Be tough and (2) be absolutely fair.

To be tough and fair a rule should (1) penalize the unfaithful, but (2) it should never penalize the faithful. Paul told Timothy, ". . . the law is made not for good men but for rebels and lawbreakers . . ." (I Tim. 1:9, NIV).

I had been tough but not fair. It was not fair to cancel the rehearsal. The people who were present were penalized for those who were not. Unfulfilled expectations produced frustration and anger. Those who came expected to rehearse. Now, I realize they should have been able to do so. It is just as tough and much more fair to make the decision of "go" or "no go" prior to the special workshop rehearsals.

Since this experience, I tell choir members that I want an absolute commitment from each of them. Either they will be at the workshop rehearsal or they will not. A card is provided for each one to register his or her intentions. The group captains are responsible to see that we have the word of every member. A tally and a decision can then be made. If a rehearsal must be canceled, it is done with the entire choir knowing it in advance. Some people might even decide to change their plans so that the choir can rehearse.

The final word is: "If you said you would be present, and you don't show up, you may expect a loving call from me, and the excuse had better be fantastic!" That is tough, but it is fair. It is working!

High requirements make issues out of musical ability, life style, attendance, and so on. I have minimum musical requirements. If a person likes to sing and is willing and able to be present, I will help develop the necessary skills. I have seen some people begin with no ability to match pitch, then develop into fine, contributing choir members. In our adult choir I won't allow a person to be a member who can't carry a tune. But I will work with the willing and determined until they can be a part of those choirs.

Having said this, I want to point out that the stiffer the requirements, the purer the group. It is like refining gold. You begin with the ore of the entire congregation as possible choir members. If the requirement level is very low as it is in most small churches,

15–20 percent of the congregation may be in the choir. In larger churches where attendance may reach beyond 2,000, for example, the requirements may be much higher, and the resulting percentage may be much smaller. How pure can you afford to make it? Shall you go for 12 karat, 14 karat or 24 karat gold?

My opinion is that until your regular singing force is steadily above 60 voices, the requirement level should remain very low. I have noticed that it becomes much easier to achieve a beautiful choral sound with volunteer singers when the size of the group reaches 60. So a choir should have at least that many, regardless of the size of the church. Of course, when a Sunday morning congregation is smaller than about 500, a singing force of 60 is virtually impossible. So if we were running above 10 percent I would feel that we were doing a good job. I have heard some fantastic 25 and 35 voice choirs. And I have seen great momentum and excitement in smaller choirs. When there is this momentum and excitement, I feel a choir will be successful regardless of the size.

Regarding life style: We allow nonchurch members to sing; but church members or not, we won't allow a person to be in choir whose life style makes what we are singing a lie.

For teenage choirs, I put it in writing. I make it precise. Just a few months ago, two of my high school choir members were dismissed because of life style violations. I told them and their parents, "When they decide to meet the standards, they will be welcomed back."

Attendance has been the most difficult area for tough, fair rule-making. But not only must rules be tough and fair, they must produce the desired results.

For routine rehearsals and services, there should be at least 75–80 percent of the active enrollment present consistently. How is this result achieved? Also, we want a happy, excited attitude in the choir. How do you get these two things happening together?

Many things I have tried have failed. I have had "excused" and "unexcused" systems. I have required various percentages. I have tried personally calling all absentees before I go home. I have tried having the group captains call all absentees. I have said, "Unless you rehearse this week, you don't sing this Sunday." There are problems with each of these policies.

I can't count the number of times I have awakened on a rehearsal day wondering and worrying whether there would be enough people to have a good rehearsal. I felt the Sunday night attendance of the teenage choir was the "pits." Unless all of them were there, it was terrible, and I was forever having some of the kids sit out, even after they had attended the Sunday afternoon rehearsal. I would try to shame them. I've gone out and dragged them up to the choir loft. I've even embarrassed them in front of the whole church by demanding, outloud, that they come from their seats by their "true love" to their seat in the choir loft.

I wouldn't still be in this work if I had not solved that one. Life is too short to endure such agony. The solution came one day during a conversation with a fellow minister of music. I asked him the same question I had asked of many others. "What sort of rules do you have for your youth choir?" What he told me clicked. Suddenly, I knew what I needed to do.

Now my mid-school and high school choir members have to accumulate at least 60 percent of the points possible to be in the year's major musical production and to go on tour. Every regular rehearsal counts 1 point. Every hour of special rehearsals counts 1 point. Every performance counts 2 points. There are no excused or unexcused absences. If you are present, you are present. If you are absent, you are absent. Sixty percent is fair. No matter what the cause, if you can't be present just a little better than half the time, you cannot do choir membership justice. That is what I tell them. I say, "You don't have to explain your absences to me. Sit out when we sing if you like. But don't come crying to me if you fall below your needed points."

I am not sure why this works so well, but it does. We publish the list of rehearsals with point values stated. We show that they can afford to lose no more than so many points. They hate to lose a point. It is not unusual for 90 percent of the kids to have 90 percent attendance. Many have 100 percent. I reward the 90 percent and above with a Director's Honor Roll party each semester.

For adults, the structure must be different, but the principle must be about the same. I have tried and failed here, too, more than I like to remember. But here is a plan a friend showed me that works for adults as well as the other works for teens. I call the rule the "four out of six, or previous performance" rule. To sing on Sunday morning, you must have been present for at least four out of the past six rehearsals or have previously performed the music. A person can't really do his or her best at less than this. Once again, four out of six is just barely better than half the time.

The enforcement is strictly "honor system." If someone is

caught violating it, then it is totally fair to confront him about it. But people seldom take advantage. The "four out of six" rule works with adults just like the "60 percent of points possible" rule works for teenagers. Actually in principle, they are identical.

In summary I would say that if you can achieve excitement and momentum, it makes it worth staying in this great work for a lifetime.

About the Contributor: *John R. Wyatt is a Baylor University graduate with a B.M. degree. He has also done post-graduate work at the University of Texas and North Texas State in Music Education. He has worked at Northway Baptist Church in Dallas, Texas, First Baptist Church in Bartlesville, Oklahoma, and is presently at Hoffmantown Baptist Church in Albuquerque, New Mexico.*

At the church in Oklahoma, John became involved in large productions, including a living Christmas tree, several civic center productions, a city-wide outdoor fourth of July celebration, and the World Premiere of the musical by Paul Johnson, "Here Comes the Son" at an annual music workshop in Waco sponsored by Word, Inc. He was also the conductor of the Phillips Symphony Orchestra in Bartlesville.

John and his family have been in Albuquerque since 1976. He says that many of the principles he began discovering in Oklahoma have also worked well in Albuquerque. In addition to his active ministry with a large and outstanding church staff, John likes to play golf and write songs.

Sonny Salsbury

2.

Beyond the Choir Loft and Back Again: Evangelism Through Music

From the editor: *How can our music reach beyond the choir loft and the church doors with the message of God's love? If we gather together to celebrate with song our new life in Christ only among ourselves, are we really doing all we can to reach other people with this good news? Among the places which music holds in the life of the family of God (worship enhancer, private worship, a common reason for gathering together) is the role of touching ears, hearts and minds of people who do not have a commitment to Jesus Christ.*

This chapter is about how a minister to youth uses a strong music program to reach beyond the church family. From choir members to their parents who come inside the church doors (for some perhaps the first time in years) to hear their son or daughter perform, to the classmates of the committed church kids, this minister's music has touched many.

In June of 1964, I attended a General Assembly of the Church of the Nazarene in Portland, Oregon. One afternoon I listened to a missionary named Paul Oriala relate his experiences in the Caribbean. Paul told of hearing some music on the way to a small chapel in the mountains where he was to conduct a service. It was coming from a group of the church young people who were singing familiar, contemporary melodies and rhythms to which they had added Christian lyrics. Paul, being a musician himself, carried this idea into his own work and soon found great success in communicating the gospel through such music. It was an important day in my life, for as I listened to Paul Oriala share his ministry, I felt that I heard God saying quietly to me, "Sonny, I want you to try the same thing here . . . in California."

As soon as I got back from Portland, I bought a guitar, asked a friend, Gary Richmond, to teach me to play it, and I began to write songs. The first song was "I've Got Something to Sing About," then "A New Song," "Psalm 19" and I had begun. I was grateful and excited to discover that God had given me the gift of composing. I was wise enough to know, however, that while I could compose, and sing well enough to be in a choir, or lead group singing, I had not been given gifts that qualified me as a performing artist. So if my songs were going to be used, I needed someone to sing them.

I thought about it, and decided, "What a great way to involve young people." So, in the fall of that year, I organized my first "contemporary youth choir." We called ourselves "The Something Singers" (after my first song), and I soon went back to my alma mater, Pasadena College, for a graduate course in choral conducting. Both the choir and I improved steadily.

As the spring of 1965 approached, I pondered, as youth director, our spring vacation activity. For years, many of the youth groups in our area had been going to Mexico for service projects. In addition to assorted manual labor, we would put on services at night, sing in English, and smile a lot.

I had always felt, as a member of those youth groups it was a little too "safe" for Christian kids like me. It wasn't too challenging to stand up for Jesus when no one knew what you were saying. As a result, when I became a youth director I decided to take our newly formed youth choir on a tour of small towns in the Mojave Desert to sing for English-speaking kids who had summer vacations, but nowhere much to go. And we prepared concerts that would speak their language.

Those were the days of the Beach Boys and the Beatles. Folk music was still popular. So we used a little of each to establish rapport, and added a number of my new songs to tell them a little about God's truth. I was most excited about the fact that my kids, including my brother Ron, were being forced into a situation of sharing their testimony in front of audiences that weren't smiling all the time, that understood exactly what was being said, and would be waiting with questions after the concert.

Well, it was great. We saw some decisions for Christ, and I

saw many choir members mature spiritually. Most of the churches I've taken choirs to have been filled with warm and welcoming Christian people. I discovered, however, that some church people who thought the concept simply wonderful for the Caribbean, didn't like it too well for the U.S.A. This became evident in the fall when we shared our trip with our area-wide church missionary convention and sang a sample of our music, "Psalm 19." We accompanied it only with one nylon string folk guitar, but created quite an uproar. "Too radical," was the cry. "The world's music doesn't belong in the church!"

Well, things progressed quickly from that point. My church's publisher, Lillenas, who in 1966 was leery of publishing my songs because they were too radical, by 1969 was at the fore of "hot" youth choir music. And the country was exploding with youth choirs.

In 1965 I knew of very few other choirs like "The Something Singers." For many years now it has been hard to find a church of any size that *doesn't* have its own youth choir. And almost all of them, sooner or later, have taken to the road. Enter the phrase "choral outreach."

Choral outreach is a coin with two sides. One side is the outreach that is accomplished *by* the choir; the other is the outreach that is accomplished *in* the choir.

When I began my career as a youth choir director, my focus was entirely on the former: the outreach accomplished through the choir. I pictured a totally dedicated band of Christian teenagers marching forth into the community and the country and wowing everyone with the gospel.

Two realities very quickly changed this picture for me. One was that my youth choir was not all "dedicated" and "mature." They were all professing Christians (that was a requirement for me *then*), but the growth and growing pains necessary for all of us made a new emphasis essential. We had to spend a lot of time admonishing, encouraging, disciplining, affirming, and so on, and the youth choir became primarily a laboratory for growing Christians and secondarily a vehicle for evangelism. This laboratory featured a great variety of experiments. Let me share a few examples.

When we were on tour, some of the kids were inclined to complain or joke about food when a host church or group served us a meal. We talked about the fact that being gracious guests would probably provide a more effective witness than any song we could ever perform.

When we were setting up for a concert, our instrumentalists would "warm up" for an unusually long time. I felt they were really showing off for the scattered kids coming around the stage. We talked about a proper response to the talents God has given us—gratitude rather than pride. And about coming out from behind the drums or the electric piano and being available to those kids, getting acquainted, and really letting them sense the love of God.

Other experiments were focused on "intra-family" relationships. Harsh words, jealousies, misunderstandings had to be acknowledged and confessed and forgiven. We learned what it meant to be accountable to each other. To get enough sleep. To study the Bible. To manage our time wisely.

The second reality dawned on me in 1969 when, after my entire lifetime (31 years) at Los Angeles First Church of the Nazarene, I moved to Yakima, Washington, and the First Presbyterian Church. I discovered that if I were to enforce the "professing Christian" requirement, I would be organizing a quartet instead of a youth choir. So I opened it up to anyone, Christian or not. We had 35 that year.

While most were not yet professing Christians, they *all* knew that Christ would be the theme of our music, and that they would continually be encouraged to follow him. Over the next eight years, our choir grew to over 100, and a great number of those choir members became Christians while they were in the choir. I rejoice in the people who have been reached by the singing of our choirs across the years (and there have been exciting stories). But I would have to say that the number of new Christians I have seen *in* the choirs have far outnumbered the new Christians won through music ministry *outside* of the choirs.

And so as I approach the subject of "evangelism through music," I would like to speak first of evangelism *within* the choir, then of that which is accomplished *by* the choir.

Evangelism within the Choir

I praise God for the many and varied tools that he has given us to accomplish his task. For me, in my particular life and ministry, the youth choir has been the greatest single tool at my disposal.

I begin the youth choir year (September) with personal interviews. These are not *auditions* in the sense that someone could be rejected on the basis of music ability. (As a matter of fact, I have had many monotones in my choirs across the years. Some have learned to sing in pitch, even read music. Others have not, but have learned to sing softly, and make up for the sound with excitement and enthusiasm.)

The interviews are a time in which I try to find out something about each person's life and interests, job, hobbies, family situation and personal faith.

Regarding families, I record parents' names and occupations, brothers' and sisters' names, ages, schools, and so on. This awareness has provided some significant outreach in itself, since church membership or association is not a prerequisite for joining.

About the only way a kid can "fail" the interview is in relation to his or her personal faith. In discussion, I learn that he or she has either already become a Christian, is not yet a Christian but is interested, or really doesn't know. In the latter case, it's often my privilege to help him or her discover a way to make a personal commitment to Jesus Christ. If, however, I were to encounter a spirit of resistance or opposition to our purpose of singing about Jesus Christ, I would feel compelled to reject that young person. I have never had to do that. Perhaps that is because by the time kids sign up for an interview with me, they know what our choir is about, and if they aren't leaning in that direction, they just don't come around.

These interviews also give me a chance to explain the requirements of the group and discuss them personally with each individual. While there have been adjustments across the years, here are our current "Celebration Company" rules and requirements. Useful tools . . . every one.

1. *Attendance.* 75 percent of all activities, choir rehearsals and performances, Bible studies, fellowship, worship, camps and retreats. This assures me that each member will be exposed to the gospel, and will witness and experience the Christian community in action, each a vital part of the church's life.

2. *"The Two of Us."* Most of the weeks in rehearsal, and every day on tours, camps and retreats, we pair off with one other person for a half hour or so. This time is spent getting better acquainted, expressing ourselves, listening and praying. Prayer partnerships are encouraged out of this experience.

3. *Reading Assignments.* Our youth choir year is September through May. I make monthly reading assignments October through May. Assigned books must be read by every member. We have often had special discussion available on more difficult

books, and frequently use the current assignments as supplemental references in Bible studies or devotional talks at fellowship meetings.

These assignments assure me that along with the barrage of messages and input our kids are getting from the media, entertainment, and their daily experience, they are getting some good solid Christian input also. Samples of books I have assigned are:

Mere Christianity by C. S. Lewis
The Hiding Place by Corrie Ten Boom
Campus Life Magazine (a current issue, cover to cover)
A Severe Mercy by Sheldon Vanauken
The Taste of New Wine by Keith Miller
Basic Christianity by Brother Andrew
The Chronicles of Narnia by C. S. Lewis (one a month)
The Screwtape Letters by C. S. Lewis

Members are strongly encouraged to buy these books, but we do provide several loan copies.

4. *Personal Testimony.* It must be understood that the lives of the choir members must not contradict or negate the group's mission. This is a flexible area, and I believe needs much discretion and wisdom on the director's part.

The best guideline for me is Scripture. If it's a clear command, enforce it. If it's not, be flexible. Not getting drunk, obeying the law, honoring parents, and so on, are clear commands. In regard to other issues, I try to reason and instruct, but do not impose a strict code of conduct where Scripture does not. For instance, alcohol is a big problem here. The Bible prohibits drunkenness, but does not prohibit drinking. The boundary line on such issues is often the opportunity to really share more deeply in the lives and struggles of my choir members.

5. *Discipline.* As a youth leader in the church, I feel I must be a combination of "a friend and a father." Now it's easy and fun to be a friend. But as a father, I must sometimes speak very sternly (after a gentle first admonition), sometimes punish, sometimes sacrifice my own popularity and acceptance.

One year in Yakima, our drummer slacked off in his Bible study and fellowship attendance. Reminders and encouragement from me resulted in no change. Everyone said, "There's no way Sonny is going to keep Jeff from going on the tour. We'd sound crummy without drums." But I did. It was a hard time. True, we didn't sound quite as good musically, and several choir members were upset with me. But it was right, and it sure had a big effect on the commitment of others over the next few years.

Rehearsal times pose a frequent discipline problem. Young people are together after several days of the school week, and it's natural to want to visit, blow off steam and goof around. It's important to have time for all those things. But not during our 1 hour and 15 minute rehearsal. While I do try to keep a light-hearted atmosphere, and occasionally inject a little humor or goofing around, I must be the one to dictate that.

When someone talks at the wrong time, my first response should be to just ask them gently and politely to quit. I feel it's important, incidentally, to call them by name, and not just address the whole choir with a general "quiet down, everybody." If a second admonition becomes necessary, it is stern. If a third, I am all father, and on occasion have kicked someone out of rehearsal. If I must do this, then I feel compelled to also get with them as soon as possible afterward and affirm them with a hug and encouragement. Even in the rehearsal, I feel it's wise, if I must speak sternly to an individual, to follow that word several minutes later with a look, smile, wink, whatever, that tells that person, "Hey, you're my friend. But I really need your help. It's forgotten. Let's keep going from here."

I believe it is important for young Christians and those who are "seeking" alike to be confronted with a loving, firm discipline in the family of God. And that, more than any other analogy, is what I see the youth choir as: a division of the Family of God.

There are several other rules and regulations, such as age, outfits, and so on which do not relate directly to outreach, and I won't mention them. But there are a few other parts of our program which are very useful tools and should be covered.

Teachable Moments

This phrase, fairly common now, was first suggested to me many years ago by Jim Slevcove, director of Emerald Cove Camp. He used it in the context of Christian camping, but it applies equally to youth choirs.

Many times a line of a lyric will raise questions, or prompt a spontaneous comment by the director. I relish such "interruptions." Maybe an ambulance siren in the distance will mark just the spot to stop and have prayer for whoever needs that ambulance, for others with physical needs, and in general. Someone coming to rehearsal late may provide the right time to say "Hey, I really appreciate you guys coming to rehearsal, even when you have some conflict and can only make part of it. But if you have to come in late, please don't attract any more attention than you can help. Just slip in quietly and join right in."

In addition to spontaneous, teachable moments, of course, we make use of regular devotional talks, in rehearsals and on tours.

Music Selection

I try to make music selection with several factors in mind, but always with the questions: "Do these lyrics serve a good purpose? If it is a Christian song, are the lyrics scriptural?" I have received dozens of letters from former choir members across the years sharing how they find themselves all the time singing old choir songs over and over as they drive, work or play. What a great opportunity—*if* the lyrics they have memorized are beneficial. What a waste and mistake if they are not. And to me if poor lyrics give a bad message to choir members, they do the same for audiences though perhaps to a lesser degree.

Evangelism Accomplished by the Choir

I hope it doesn't sound like a cop out, but to me the most effective evangelism ever to be achieved by any youth choir by far will result from a harmonious, supportive nonexclusive growing love among the members of that choir. The most dynamic, electric performance *on* stage means nothing when contradicted by the choir's words and behavior off the stage.

I have hosted a number of professional Christian groups across the years, as well as nonprofessional youth choirs and groups. These experiences, together with fifteen years of taking my own gang on the road have led to this partial list of suggestions for effective "outreach" through music.

1. Being tired and exhausted hinders the ministry of any human being, and can be avoided, contrary to popular belief. I once heard a wise word in a sermon: "When a Christian is tired, the most Christian thing he or she can do is go to sleep."

I therefore try to plan my tours with adequate time for sleep and relaxation, so the choir can give themselves fully when they are "on," in personal relationships with each other, with audiences before and after concerts, and as guests in homes.

And I have discovered that high school folks need to be reminded that it is not just "their business" if they want to stay up late. The resulting ill temper will affect everyone, as will the increased chance of illness.

2. Youth choirs can have a great outreach just by being gracious guests. This includes never complaining about a meal's quality, quantity or frequency (we once had 10 fried chicken meals in 9 days), courtesy in homes, making beds, leaving bathrooms clean, following the host's lead as far as bedtime and breakfast time, as well as leaving thank-you notes in their rooms.

3. Nonverbal communication is an extremely important factor in effective outreach. Experts tell us that 85 to 90 percent of what is communicated, whether from the stage, in a small group, or one on one, is communicated nonverbally. That makes it very important for choirs to smile on happy songs, be involved and sincere on serious songs, look and listen when someone is speaking, look into the eyes of the audience as they are singing (unless they are supposed to be following the director on a song.)

4. Flexibility is an important quality to encourage. To minister with one song when you're prepared to do an hour, or vice versa, can be a disaster or a great witness. The deciding factor between disaster and witness is often how flexible the choir is in having a gracious attitude about changes. I believe this realization is basic to the concept of the Christian as a *servant.*

5. Every choir member should have an assignment besides his or her musical participation, like: sound system, set-up, bus clean-up, first aid kit, outfit ironing, instrumental tuning, and so on. I make these assignments not just so that these important tasks get done, but also so that the members develop responsibility and a sense of serving.

6. I have almost always shied away from concerts where neither I nor the host church knows what to expect, as far as evangelical stance, type of music, purpose of the concert, and so on. As I mentioned earlier, most churches have received us with loving enthusiasm. But once I called a church the day before we were to arrive for a concert to verify details. They had just received the posters which had been delayed in the mail. Seeing the "long hair" on some of the boys, and the electric guitar and drums among the group (this had been verified on the phone and in writing), they wanted to cancel. I told them I had 75 kids whom they were honor bound to house and feed that next night, whether or not we sang.

When we arrived, we left all our instruments on the bus and sang an a capella concert. For our group, that was a great "teachable moment," subject: "flexibility." Our responsibility to serve those people outweighed our customary musical procedure. I have never been interested in a crusade for a certain style of music. The only crusade is Christ. I don't really know if we accomplished anything for those people, but it was a growing experience for our choir. And it convinced me once and for all that more can be accomplished in outreach endeavors when both the choir and the hosts know where the other is coming from.

7. I believe strongly that concerts aimed at non-Christian audiences are most effective when they include a few familiar, secular songs. Many choirs and groups believe that contemporary rhythm and instrumentation of their Christian songs will accomplish a sense of rapport with a secular audience. It will help. But in my opinion, a familiar song, done well, does more. That's why we learn "A Bicycle Built for Two," and "Won't You Come Home, Bill Bailey?" when we go regularly to convalescent homes. It says, "These young people care about us. They identify." The same is probably true, I think, with any audience.

I strongly reject the concept that this is using the "world's music." Christ is the creator of all things, including music. So the world is using music, a creation of God's, for its own design, and in wrong ways in many cases. To me, using a "secular" song as part of a musical evangelistic effort is merely claiming another part of God's creation to be used for his glory.

I recently used "United We Stand" as a Sunday morning anthem by our youth choir. I received a protest letter for this, with the complaint that it was used as a commercial tune for United Airlines and so familiar in a secular context that it was therefore unfit for sacred worship. My response is that the lyrics are based on Scripture, it fit wonderfully with the theme of that morning, and the familiarity, instead of being a liability, was actually an asset. Every time our people heard that ad in the weeks to come, it could remind them about the unity we have in Christ's family, and about which we had sung in church.

8. Whenever the spoken word is used in a concert, whether it is by the director or a choir member, and whether the person is introducing a song or expressing a personal testimony or preaching, he or she should try to avoid certain pitfalls. Some speeches are too smooth, sound canned and obviously memorized (rather than being spontaneous). On the other hand, a more common pitfall is to ramble, stray from the subject, get long winded, and repeat oneself. I cringe when I hear a testimony start off with, "Well, I don't know what I'm going to say, but here goes." It

might prove interesting, but probably won't be profitable. While I think it is fine to mention an exciting or humorous incident, I believe testimonies should have Christ and the Christian experience as their central theme. As far as we choir directors are concerned, I agree with Christian recording artist Larry Norman: being musicians does not necessarily qualify us to be preachers.

9. Finally, I believe members of youth choirs should have as clear an understanding of their faith as possible and those who are Christians should be capable of possibly leading someone else to Christ themselves. I think Peter 3:15 is the premiere verse on witnessing in the entire Bible. "Be prepared to give an answer to everyone who asks you to give the reason for the hope that you have." It is an important responsibility of the choir director to help the choir members feel this readiness.

To me the most exciting chance to share is with a fellow choir member. And some of the most solid Christians I have known have been young people who joined our youth choir as interested "seekers," and then became Christians in the warmth of a community where they had seen Christianity in action. I still think this is choral outreach at its best.

In closing, I must confess that in a way, I have come full circle regarding choral outreach. In 1979 I moved back to California to La Jolla Presbyterian Church, and in the spring of 1980, I took my youth choir on our annual spring tour to, of all places, Mexico. We did some smiling, laughing, and playing soccer and tag. We also sang, but not in English. We sang "Breakfast in Galilee" in its entirety in Spanish. It was effective outreach. At the Boys' Prison in Mexicali, nine young men received Christ. Since Mexico is right in our back yard here in the San Diego area, how can we deny our responsibility?

We also sang it in several Spanish speaking churches in Los Angeles, and because of that week, many doors are now open to us for further ministry *en español.* Los Angeles is *currently* Spanish speaking to the tune of 48 percent. By the end of this decade, Spanish will be the predominant language among the population of the state of California. Somehow, I feel God is leading us into a new opportunity of outreach.

Muchas gracias. Adios. Vaya con Dios.
(Thank you very much. Good-by. God go with you!)

About the Contributor: *Sonny Salsbury has a B.A. degree from Pasadena College and has served as minister to youth in several churches, including First Church of the Nazarene in Los Angeles, and First Presbyterian Church of Yakima, Washington. Sonny is now at La Jolla Presbyterian Church in La Jolla, California, where he directs an educational, social, recreational and spiritual program for the junior high through college age people in the church.*

Sonny also worked on the staff of the Los Angeles Youth for Christ (Campus Life) from 1960 to 1964 and has published an article called "Why Do We Sing?" in the Journal of Christian Camping.

Sonny was on the cutting edge of the contemporary church music scene in the 1960s with his youth group called "The Electric Church," and composed several anthems, including "The Father Loves You," "Here Comes Jesus" and "Psalm 19" which are still used in churches today. He served on the committee which compiled the first volume of "Sing 'n' Celebrate" and has been influential in Christian youth music ever since.

As a composer, Sonny has continued to write and has written several youth musicals, including a Christmas musical, "Love Came Down," and two others: "Backpacker's Suite" and "Breakfast in Galilee," published by Word Music. His other interests include antiques, backpacking, home decorating and sports. He and his wife, Linda, live in La Jolla, California.

E. Martene Craig

3.

Special Projects—Where Does the Money Come From?

From the editor: I've heard ministers of music say that there are people in their congregations who don't believe that a music program should cost anything. And there is nothing that throws cold water on dreaming up a vital and motivating ministry more than the feeling of not having the money to carry it out.

One approach which seems to produce results is that of dreaming as if the money would be available . . . seeing just how a really effective music project could be planned. Presenting a specific project designed to minister in a specific way seems to draw a more favorable response from budget committees than just asking for money for "general music purposes."

This chapter is about a minister of music who saw that her church music budget couldn't support the plans she had made, but she didn't give up. She planned big without letting the lack of money stop the dreams. Then the practical part of finding out what the project would cost was easier. How she came to the place where the church music committee voted an extra $10,000 in her annual music budget is an informative and inspiring story.

There are two scriptures which are to me the core of my commitment to a ministry in music. One is from Jesus—the Great Commission (Matt. 28:19,20 KJV): "Go ye therefore, and teach all nations, baptizing them in the name of the Father, and of the Son, and of the Holy Ghost: Teaching them to observe all things whatsoever I have commanded you. And lo, I am with you alway, even unto the end of the world." He said that we are to *teach*.

The other is from the Apostle Paul, who told us in Colossians 3:16 (KJV), "Let the word of Christ dwell in you richly in all wisdom; teaching and admonishing one another in psalms and hymns and spiritual songs, singing with grace in your hearts to the Lord." For me, this scripture is actually the music ministry in a nutshell just as John 3:16 is the gospel in a nutshell.

As I thought about these two scriptures, I began also to think about ways I might apply this to the music programs for which I was responsible. But after every dreaming session I seemed always to come back to the same point: the need for the financial support to carry out the dreams.

Some Basic Funding Sources which Already Existed

As our outreach programs began to develop, I saw the funds also develop from some very loving, generous, committed people. Some of our pieces of equipment for sound, lighting and multimedia, and musical instruments like electric pianos, and synthesizers were donated by some of these people. Other items were purchased from a special music fund to which many more people contributed. And we bought some things from the funds in the music budget of the church.

The upkeep of the equipment is done by the generous help of our lay people. Some of the equipment is built specifically for our needs, like the music stand with a communications system in it that was built for me. Since I direct from the location of the instrumentalists, it is impossible to know if the balance is correct in other parts of the room. The sound engineer can let me know through the communication system if a particular instrument is too loud or too soft and if the vocalists are at the right level. It is so exciting for me to see talented men and women give their service to Christ in ways like this. The music ministry involves a lot more than music.

Any additions or replacement of equipment are put into the budget and from time to time there are private donations that help take care of very needy areas. All of the choirs and vocal groups operate on the basis of a faith ministry. If it is possible to take up a free will offering, then we use this money to pay for expenses, especially in our local area.

Our music budget, however, was clearly not adequate for our music ministry, and the church as a whole did not seem aware that we needed a larger part of the overall budget to be the kind of outreaching music department I believe Jesus and Paul want us to be.

Funding a Special Dream

One of my dreams was to develop an outreach to our whole community. Christmas seems to be one special time that can be a meaningful experience for people both within the church family and without, so we planned an outreach dream around this season. To give you an idea of the amount of financial support we needed, let me describe the reality the dream has become.

Each Christmas, all of the choirs, and in fact the entire church, work on our Annual Round-the-Table Carol Sings that are presented seven times during December at the Los Angeles County Fairgrounds. We take an empty building and convert it into "Christmas." There is a huge snow scene across one end with an ice skating rink and ice skaters, a toboggan run with toboggans and a ski slope with skiers. We also have a screen at that end with stars behind it which shine through and are lit up at different times.

At the opposite end is a huge stained glass window with the handbell choirs in front of it and two huge Christmas trees, one on either side, that have lights on them like a color organ—they go on and off when the bells are played. On either side of the trees are the Living Masters—famous paintings which we have depicted using real people. They look like paintings you might see at the Laguna Art Festival.

On the other two sides of the room facing each other are bleachers for the choirs. On one side are the youth choirs—junior high, high school and college-career choirs. Opposite these choirs are the children's choir, the primary and junior choirs and the adult choir. Above the choirs are huge multi-media screens on which we project the words of carols that the people sing, and also multi-images.

In the center of the room, the people are seated around tables. We can seat over 1,500 people at one performance. The choirs sing together, individually and sometimes echo back and forth. Small groups sing in the snow scene, handbell choirs play, the orchestra accompanies and plays a beautiful overture and candlelighters light the candles on the tables. After the flaming figgy pudding comes in, the food is served—hot wassail and figgy pudding!

It takes hundreds of people to prepare for this event, and it takes hundreds to participate, but God has used this to attract many to him and to bring many into our fellowship.

As I completed my early plans for this dream, I saw that the cost of doing something which will really reach people can be greater than the average member of the congregation may realize. Of course, many companies and individuals donated materials and know-how, and these are carefully listed in the program each year. And as I said, we try to cover expenses by taking offerings at our concerts. Down through the years, however, people began to feel that this was not the best way to finance the carol sings. Many of them were inviting their friends and they did not want to have an offering taken. So we decided to sell tickets for this and one other function, Singsation, which are held away from the church. Other reasons for doing this included being able to control the number of people at each presentation, and having reserved seats to eliminate the long lines and the problems that had developed from people trying to save seats

The tickets had been a nominal charge: $1.00 for Singsation and $3.00 for Carol Sings. In almost every instance this has not covered expenses. In fact this year the Carol Sing tickets will have to be raised to $4.00 due to the tremendous increase in all costs. This is still a very nominal charge, I feel.

Funding Bigger Dreams

All of the income sources I have mentioned so far were meeting our needs for the projects that "didn't take much money," the ones we did in our own local area. These included singing concerts in parks, beaches, shopping centers, prisons, hospitals, rallies, churches, television, military bases, local schools or local theaters (like Singsation). These ministries use all of the elementary age through college-career choirs, puppets, orchestra, drama, and of course all of the production crews needed for lighting, staging, sound and multimedia.

But the outreach programs that involved traveling really required a larger amount of money than the local programs. When the junior high, high school and college-career choirs went on such tours, they often paid for the transportation and some of the food themselves. We try to get lodging and the rest of the food from organizations in the areas where we go.

In the past years, there have been fund-raising projects to bring down the cost for each individual. There have been car washes, rummage sales, slave days where the young people were hired out by members of the congregation to do different jobs, can collections, bottle collections, pizza sales, candy sales, and card sales. These would bring in some money to help with the expenses.

The big fund-raising projects, however, were the ones that the Overtones (a small audition group out of the college-career choir) undertook to support their overseas or cross-country ministries. The first and most successful one was the Bike-a-thon.

A Bike-a-thon is an event in which choir members (and any interested friends) ride their bicycles along a designated route for a certain number of miles. There are various checkpoints along the way where bike riders stop, have their entry card stamped, get a drink of water, rest if they need to, then continue on the route. The ride ends at a city park where the Overtones present an outdoor concert.

Those who ride in the Bike-a-thon get sponsors who pay them a certain amount of money per mile for each mile they can ride. This money is then paid by the sponsors to the choir fund earmarked for the particular tour we are planning.

The event itself is worth doing because of several good effects of its own. (1) The kids in the choir make contact with potential sponsors, letting people know about the outreach program. (2) The riders get a good healthy workout. (3) The feeling of riding for a purpose—to earn the means to share the message of God's saving grace with others—creates a special "oneness" among the choir members. (4) The afternoon concert gives the choir some more singing experience and the listeners a meaningful experience as well. It is itself an outreach program for the community, as well as a fund-raising project.

Procedures for a Bike-a-thon

For our first Bike-a-thon, sponsored by the Overtones, each member of the choir who participated was eligible to receive money from the proceeds for his or her expenses on the tour. Each member was given instructions in how to talk to sponsors, valuable information for relations with people later on. The instructions I gave the participants are listed here:

Suggestions to Riders
Overtones' Bike-a-thon—April 3, 1976

How to Fill Out Sponsor Sheets:

1. Fill out the information from each sponsor on the reverse side of this sheet. Don't forget to get your sponsor's signature.
2. Copy all information from this sheet onto the Official List of Sponsors.
3. Do not lose either sponsor sheet! You will be asked to turn in the Official List of Sponsors at the starting checkpoint. Keep this sponsor sheet to collect your pledges.

How to Get Sponsors:

1. Visit businesses in your area, go door to door, ask your parents to get their friends and people at their work; get your best friend to ride with you and also get sponsors; ask your teachers, relatives, anyone and everyone.
2. Write a letter to your friends and relatives who live elsewhere and ask them to sponsor you for so many miles and to send their money as soon as possible after the Bike-a-thon.

Make a Good Impression:

1. Etiquette, enthusiasm and good grooming are the key to selling our cause. Smile *and* be enthusiastic.
2. Good grooming is a must. Dress as you would for church. It will help make a positive first impression.
3. Good manners are very important for a good witness.
   (1) Don't forget to say "please" and "thank you."
   (2) If they decide not to help sponsor, give them a concert ticket anyway and ask them to come to the Overtones' Concert—to be held at Ganesha Park Bandshell at the end of the ride (3:30 P.M.)

On the reverse side of this instruction sheet is their personal sponsor sheet with columns for them to fill in the date, name, address, phone, cents per mile, comments and to get the signature of each sponsor. A rider can enter with as many sponsors as he or she can sign up in advance of the ride.

We did a lot of advertising in the church and in the community. Brochures were given out to as many people as possible. The bicycle routes were mapped out, and the checkpoints were established so that the riders could get their cards stamped to show that they had ridden the proper number of miles. People were enlisted to serve at the checkpoints.

One result was that many families rode together, and it was a great day of fellowship and wonderful exercise. Since bicycling is one of my favorite sports, I really got involved myself. I rode the forty miles, and even though the last seven miles was in a downpour of rain, I was bound and determined to complete the ride. I received a plaque with an old-fashioned bicycle on it and an inscription. The second year, I did fifty miles and both times brought in over $800 for the outreach.

The concert scheduled by the group in the afternoon in the park brought the day to a climax. This was not only an outreach to the community but also an opportunity for the community and church to see the group that they were supporting.

By the end of our first Bike-a-thon we found we had raised over $8,000 in all, and everyone had such an enjoyable day. We had so much fun, in fact, that people who were physically not able to ride bicycles such a distance wanted us to find a way to include them too!

So a year later, we added rocking chairs to the events of the day, and called the event a Bike-a-Rock. Many senior adults became involved and had a great time. They brought their rocking chairs to the bandstand where the concert was going to be in the afternoon, and there they rocked. People sponsored them for so much money a minute. This was even more successful than the year before, bringing in $10,000 in one Saturday. We started riding and rocking at 8:00 A.M. and concluded with the concert at 3:30 P.M. in the park.

The Effect of the Success on the Church

The Bike-a-thon and the Bike-a-Rock were a huge success. We even had local stores make awards available to the people bringing in the most money. Because of our huge success other groups in the church wanted to do more and more fund-raising projects. The Board of Deacons was faced with a deluge of requests—many other kinds of fund-raising activities different from our Bike-a-Rock. They found themselves in the awkward position of having to say "yes" to some projects but "no" to most of them. The groups who were turned down would ask why the music ministry was allowed to raise funds while they were not.

After a great deal of consideration and prayer, the Board of Deacons voted that there would be no more fund-raising projects. But the good news came when they then recommended to the Board of Trustees that the same amount of money previously made from the Bike-a-Rock be designated for the music budget, and so $10,000 was put into the outreach ministry of the music department! The only fund-raising projects now permissible are those where individuals want to do jobs for other people. It is felt that we could still have our young people do work for those who wanted to hire them, and the young person could keep the money to pay for his or her expenses on tour.

Although we miss the fun and excitement of doing the Bike-a-Rock, I am grateful that the Board of Trustees now sees our need for large amounts of money. And we can now spend our time on the main tasks of planning the outreach programs themselves.

Wider Outreach Dreams Now Funded

How do we use these sums of money? Here are just a few of the many experiences I have personally witnessed as a direct result of our outreach programs. And if I had allowed my dreams to be cut short or limited by the lack of funds, many of these might never have happened.

The junior high choir takes an outreach tour on a weekend to San Diego, the coastal, desert area, and presents the gospel in churches, shopping centers, military bases and so on. The high school group goes during Easter week to Arizona, the San Francisco area, Oregon, or Nevada and they make presentations to many places that do not often receive groups. Last year they toured an Indian reservation. There had not been a group like this on that reservation for four or five years, and God used us in a mighty way.

The college-career group also goes on a long weekend in February to some of the closer areas. For example, one winter they were in the Las Vegas area and sang in shopping centers, prisons, juvenile delinquent homes, churches and military bases. Each summer the Overtones, the college-career small audition group, travels for four to six weeks. Some of the outreach trips they have made are: Alaska, Australia, New Zealand, Fiji, Hawaii, Japan, Taiwan, Korea, Hong Kong, the Philippines, and across America. They sing in schools, military bases, churches, prisons, hospitals, and wherever the Lord opens the door.

From time to time it has been difficult to get the instrumentalists whom we have needed for our tours, so we have used someone who may not be a Christian. In practically every instance that person has made a commitment to Christ before the outreach ministry was over.

One young man made a personal commitment to Christ in Hawaii and has continued the past several years in the music ministry. In fact, at present he is on the road with a Christian music group. Another young man dropped in on a rehearsal and realized that the people here had something he didn't have, and he wanted it too. He talked with one of the members following the rehearsal. Later that night, he knelt in his room and made a commitment to Christ. He has attended the group rehearsals regularly ever since and has been growing by leaps and bounds in his new life.

Many members of the choir have made new or renewed commitments to Christ during an outreach ministry, and it seems to be because they are confronted over and over with what they are singing while presenting the gospel to others. Some of these are people who have been raised in the church, but have never made a commitment themselves. Some are from homes where no one in the family has made a commitment to Christ, and a friend has brought them to choir.

One of the most exciting and rewarding experiences happened recently when one of the groups was touring in Australia. They played sports during the day with students from a girls' college. That night after the concert by the group, fifty-one girls committed their lives to Christ.

One college-career young person wrote from an outreach ministry in the South Pacific,

> I am so much more in tune to the Holy Spirit's leading than I have ever been before. He is giving me such a boldness. It sure isn't me! I still have a long way to go, but it's coming and I'm willing to give my best for the Lord! I'm just an ordinary person, but God uses ordinary people. "I Give Him All," and that's what matters. That song is really ministering to me this tour . . . also "Fly Like an Eagle" has such terrific words! Especially, "Flying with the strength of our youth. Waiting for the Lord we'll gain new strength and we'll run without tiring as we trust in the Lord." Isn't that neat?

When financial shortages seem about to halt our plans, I have found that the Lord has given me ideas on how to overcome these shortages, the courage to dare to try a new large plan, the support and ability from a talented staff, and the belief that "we can do all things through him who strengthens us." The times the choirs, the music staff and I have worked together toward a solution to our financial needs have been rewarding, challenging, and uplifting. And we have been drawn together into closer, more meaningful relationships, by supporting each other, than any of us could have imagined!

About the Contributor: *E. Martene Craig administrates a music department of over 1,200 participants and 25 groups, including members from preschool age through senior adult. She has been at First Baptist Church in Pomona, California, since 1969. Before* *that, Martene studied at Baldwin-Wallace Conservatory of Music in Berea, Ohio, and Western Reserve University in Cleveland, Ohio. She graduated from Moody Bible Institute in Chicago, Illinois, and went on to receive a B.A. in Music from California State University at Fullerton, California. She has also studied at Redlands University, University of California at Riverside, California State University at Long Beach, and California Baptist Seminary.*

She served as minister of music at First Baptist Church in Colton, California, then as Director of Christian Education and Music at First Baptist Church, Fullerton, California, before going to Pomona.

Martene is also staff clinician for Lexicon Music of Woodland Hills, California, and has led seminars at workshops on the subjects of "The Graded Choir Program," "Children's Choirs," "Youth Choirs," "Choreography," "Working with Your Pastor," and various other subjects. She has led repertoire reading sessions in music for all age groups and some of her choral groups have participated in recordings such as "The Enchanted Journey," a children's musical by Cam and Cher Floria recorded by Light Records, one of Lexicon Music's record labels.

Her resourcefulness, dedication, and boundless energy have endeared her to thousands of people whose lives she has touched throughout her ministry.

Mack M. Moore

4.

Good News for Volunteer Choir Directors!

From the editor: *Many churches do not have the money to hire a full-time, or even a part-time, professionally trained minister of music. Other churches find themselves "in between" ministers of music, and need someone to lead the choir and other music in the worship service on Sundays until a full-time person can be found.*

If you have found yourself in the role of choir director, perhaps feeling a little uneasy because you haven't had the "benefit" of a music education, I think you'll find the hope, reassurance, and practical advice you may have been looking for in this chapter.

You've just met the last "well-wisher," having become a new member of the church. You joined this particular church because you feel it is a place where God can "put you to work." Your new hometown is small, and the church membership is less than other churches of which you have been a part. Yet, even with a smaller congregation and a church staff of only the pastor and a church secretary, you feel an excitement in the air—a thrill of entering into a new era of special service to the Lord! Little do you know what's coming next . . .

The pastor, approaching you with a smile, tells you how happy he is that you have come to be a part of the "family." He also pointedly states that he would really love to see you involved in the music ministry of the church, perhaps in a leadership capacity. (You were already aware that it was he who announced and directed the congregational singing.) You hear him say, "With your excellent background in music training and performance"—(high school and college chorus plus private piano lessons for seven years!)—"I believe you are the very one to build us a number one, class-A music program here in our church." And, relying on God's leadership and your desire to be put to work, you hear yourself accepting this position. "Dear Lord, where in the world do we go from here?"

I think I might be able to share with you some ideas which could aid you in your new field of service. I am not an authority on the matter of organizing and working with the volunteer choral program, but through the years, my inexcusable mistakes have taught me a great deal that I would like to pass on to others. I hope my advice will spare them similar agony and mistakes.

Take a Look Around

It will be helpful, I think, to find out if an organized choral program has ever been functional at the church. If so, who were its leaders and how many choral groups were a part of that organization? You might find invaluable help from those who helped to lead in a previous choral program. But then again, you might best "start from scratch" after listening and thinking about that previous leader's contribution, if you get my drift! It is amazing how so many volunteer choral programs in churches have dwindled to nothing with such "outstanding" leadership!

Look for a good rehearsal room that you can use for practice, storage of music and equipment—and one that can be available to you and your choir at the times you will need it. If you can get one reserved for nothing but the choir, that is ideal. Perhaps you are fortunate enough to have a room already designated as the choir room. You might even be *unfortunate* to have one designated! In this case, I suggest you use your naiveté and "being new on the scene" to the fullest. Relocate, if at all possible, should the room not be one that can fulfill the needs of you and your group. And establish that room as the choir's place as your ministry begins. I have noticed many times that change is a bit more readily accepted early in one's time of service.

Other factors to consider in your look around are: Who will you be working with? How many people are involved in the choir program at this time? Are there any others with potential who can add to the choir's size and musical ability?

I want to add quickly here that it seems wise to me to *be willing to start small, think big, pray hard and grow toward your aspirations.* Remember that neither Rome nor the Mormon Tabernacle Choir was built in a day! It is better to begin with one choir and successfully develop it rather than have three or four mediocre struggling groups. Mediocrity attracts only those who are satisfied with less than the best. Success in your choral program will draw interested and talented people to your church, which will allow you to have an even larger program and perhaps pave the way for professional leadership.

Accompanists can make or break a music ministry. Consider the present accompanist and determine in your own mind whether or not a change would benefit your ministry. I am all too aware that this doesn't always settle the matter. If Miss Sadie has played the organ for the church since the Chicago fire and doesn't want to give up the job, carefully weigh the consequences of asking her to consider another position within the church's music program. Usually, relatives and good friends of Miss Sadie fill not only the church roll, but every major board and committee of the church! What is to be done then?

To me, the best overall solution is to befriend Miss Sadie. Try to sincerely show her love and appreciation for what she has done and is doing. After all, she is serving the Lord in her way to the best of her ability. Let her know that her position of service is not threatened. Who knows? If you didn't have Miss Sadie, you might not have anyone else who could play any better. Or, you could find yourself with a prima donna at the keyboard who couldn't care less if the Lord is being honored, or *much* less if your leadership and wishes are being followed. For many people, playing the organ at a church is merely a job to do.

Even with the limited abilities of Miss Sadie, through loving her and caring for her, I believe she can be helped to be a better accompanist.*

Should Miss Sadie be unable to play the more difficult pieces on the level you feel appropriate for presentation in the worship service, your music publisher and some recording companies can come to your rescue! More and more accompaniment tapes are becoming available for many selections, both in collection form and in single copy form. These not only provide excellent orches-

---

* Chapter 17 by Owen Griffin about "What Accompanists Wish Choir Directors Knew" can give you some insight about the feelings of a person in that role, even though Miss Sadie may not be musically all that Owen is.

trated accompaniment, but I think they often set a worshipful mood through tastefully recorded music that could never have been achieved with the standard instruments in the worship service.

In addition, there are good accompaniment tapes for the vocal soloist, featuring many favorite Christian solo selections. These are usually on cassette tape, while choral tapes come on reel-to-reel or cassette. Both of these taped accompaniment forms can be ordered through most religious book stores, Christian music stores, or directly from the publishers.*

Another answer to poor accompaniment on some numbers is to try the number unaccompanied! Good a cappella singing by the choir or vocal ensemble is a favorite creative way to get around poor accompaniment. I would attempt this only with a group that can readily sing parts unaccompanied with no pitch or tonal quality difficulties. It is a toss up as to which is more difficult to endure in a captive audience like a church worship service—poor accompaniment or poor a cappella singing!

After a time, Miss Sadie might come to realize that she is falling short in accomplishing what the worship service needs instrumentally. Since you have shown her love and Christian caring, she might be able to gracefully step aside to allow a ministry to develop which she otherwise would be holding back. Come what may, yours will have been a relationship in Christian love that was valuable to both you and Miss Sadie. You both have grown in Christ. And, isn't that what being a Christian is all about?

What Do We Sing?—When Do We Sing It?—and Who Sings It?

After determining the level of your choir's ability and keeping in mind the limitations of your accompaniment, you are now ready to choose the music for your church.

I still practice in my present church what I did in my days as a student minister of music in smaller churches. I pray daily for guidance in choosing material that will present the good news of Jesus Christ to both the person who is moved by the stateliest of anthems and the fellow whose richest spiritual experience musically is the singing of the sweet chorus, "Alleluia, Alleluia."

With the variety of materials available to churches today, there are few excuses for anyone to leave a worship service saying that

---

* More details about this whole area of using taped accompaniments can be found in Chapter 11.

the music left him or her cold. We must minister to *all* the people, and you, as a member of your church will know best what they respond to. I cannot say strongly enough that it should be what *they* respond to—not what *you* respond to. True, through our ministries, we can educate and cultivate a "better taste" or "wider acceptance" of music. But that is not why God called us. I believe your calling and mine are the same, volunteer part-time or full-time minister of music: to share the good news of Jesus Christ so that others may find him as Savior and Lord.

And it follows that if this is our calling, the music we choose for use in worship must reflect this message. We must try not to allow the "beat" of a number, the accompaniment of a song, a taped recording, to become the focal point. The *words* and *message* are the most vital parts of the music we use.

Simple Choir Selections from the Hymnal

If you have to work with an extremely limited budget, there are ways to create innovative worship experiences and choral activities using only the hymnal. Beautifully moving choral offerings can be arranged by having your choir hum softly one verse of a hymn while a soloist sings the melody line. Another verse could be done in unison with specially arranged accompaniment if your pianist or organist can comply. Or you might alternate your ladies and your men singing the two middle verses of the hymn.

Another idea is to use an instrumental soloist, such as a violinist, flutist, or trumpeter, to play alone on one verse; then, join the choir on the last verse. High school level band or orchestra students (or college level if there is a university in your town) can handle this level of music.*

Sometimes I have tried using two or more hymns, related both in theme and key, to form a medley. One arrangement that I like uses "Jesus, Keep Me Near the Cross" and "When I Survey the Wondrous Cross" together. "Amazing Grace" coupled with "Grace Greater Than Our Sin" also makes a very moving medley.

Beyond the Hymnal—The Music Library

Is there a semblance of a music library? Perhaps predecessors or industrious choir members have seen fit to provide a makeshift means of filing and caring for church music. However, in most

---

* Other ways to use instrumental players are described in Chapter 7.

cases, I am sorry to relate, an all-out appeal is necessary to gather in church hymnals, copies of sheet music, copies of octavo selections, chorus books, and so on, which belong to the church, but through the years have found their way to the bottom of piano benches throughout the community. After the monumental task of harvesting all of this material, it then must be separated, processed and filed, using the best system you can adapt for your particular situation.

I have developed a card filing system with several ways to cross-index, which I shall describe here. To get it set up and operating may take some extra volunteer help from choir members, and some administration and just plain clerical work on your part, but after the hard part comes the good part—you can locate pieces of music suitable for various occasions. You can know whether a particular anthem has been used in the recent past. You can locate seasonal, patriotic, and other topical items more quickly than without this system.

The filing system I use is centered around three major divisions or categories: (1) Octavos (sometimes called anthems), (2) Cantatas/Oratorios/Collections (Books of music for choirs) and (3) Vocal/Instrumental Solos/Ensembles. After sorting out all of the music into these three categories, use a numbering system beginning with OCT 001, COC 001, and SE 001. Always make certain each copy is stamped with the name and address of the church, as well as the filing number.

For storing music, I prefer storage boxes, showing the filing number and the title of the selection. Lined up on open shelves or in cabinets, they make the music easily available as well as protect it from dust and weather. These boxes are available from most music dealers. If enough shelving is not available, however, 10″ x 12″ pocket type envelopes with clasps may be used and stored in a filing cabinet. Separate drawers, rather than shelves, can be designated OCT, COC, or SE. The music would be filed numerically.

I use a three-card filing system for cataloging the music. Music stores, book stores and music publishers are some places to get these cards. One publishing company always includes cards for processing the music along with the music shipment. The three-card system which I set up, however, uses different colors as a filing aid, so the cards must be purchased from a religious book and supply store.

One colored card is called the *title card,* and is filed by title alphabetically. Another is the *composer card* and is filed by the last name of the composer and/or arranger alphabetically. The final card is the *numerical card.* It is filed under one of several categories, always in numerical sequence. This is a boon in special service planning for seasonal or other emphases within the church. The categories include:

Hymn Arrangement
General Anthem
Easter
Christmas
Thanksgiving
Communion
Evangelistic
Youth
Patriotic

Since it is possible to use a selection for several different occasions or types of services, the numerical card is filed several times. For example, the arrangement of "When I Survey the Wondrous Cross" by Mallory could be found under "Hymn Arrangement," "Easter" and "Communion" headings. "If We Don't Make It Work, Who Will?" by Buryl Red is found under both "Youth" and "Patriotic" headings.

These cards are kept in card file boxes at my fingertips for fast reference. They give the title, composer and/or arranger, publisher, publisher's copy number, and the degree of difficulty of the piece. They also tell if the number is a gospel solo, hymn arrangement, Thanksgiving anthem, and so on.

There is a space on the card to indicate the number of copies on hand, which was determined when the music was first sorted and filed. Nothing can be more aggravating than to plan to do a particular piece only to find you are short a number of copies. Another very helpful feature of the cards is space on the back where the dates the piece was used can be written. This prevents using the number again within too short a length of time.

Another idea is a master copy notebook, which is a real help. One copy of each octavo and collection/oratorio/cantata is punched and placed in looseleaf notebooks in numerical order. A master list of all vocal/instrumental solo/ensemble numbers also in numerical order, is included in this notebook. As my library grew, I added volumes of these notebooks. How much easier it is to locate a number for quick review in these notebooks than to pour over box after box of music, or to resort to relying on an extremely poor memory.*

* Developing a balanced choral library is discussed in greater detail by John Purifoy in Chapter 5.

Planning

Equally important to choosing music for a church is scheduling the presentation of that music. Not only is it good for you as a minister of music to know what is coming up to help you plan rehearsals, but it's also a good idea for your choir to be able to know when future numbers are scheduled to be sung.

I try to plan three months at a time both anthem and solo/ ensemble presentations. After making up a calendar, a copy of the schedule is given to each choir member and the pastor. Conscientious members use this schedule as a guide to plan necessary weekend travel. And, unless absolutely necessary, no changes are made in this schedule. The pastor has told me he really appreciates knowing what is going to be sung and who will be participating in solos or in ensembles.

Guest Choirs and Artists

Not only is it wise to schedule in advance the music to be used, but I also try to expose the members to as many individuals and groups from outside the church membership as possible. Don't get me wrong. I am *most* selective in choosing those who come to minister to the people in my church. We are not interested in having *performances,* but rather in being *ministered to.*

The credentials of those who come to sing are carefully examined. Unless they are highly recommended by a person whom I know and whose opinion I value highly, or unless I personally know the individual or group, they are not invited to lead us in worship. I seek to use people who will bless our people with the message of Jesus Christ and his love. You can invite visiting choirs from respected music departments of colleges, universities, and even certain high schools, as well as youth choirs and adult choirs from neighboring churches, to come and sing.

Choirs of outstanding abilities inspire and uplift us spiritually. They also encourage the people to try to keep growing and improving musically and spiritually. The choir members are able to hear firsthand the correct use of good tonal quality, the use of dynamics and the good enunciation we often talk to them about but cannot seem to get across.

Usually, a love offering is the only financial expectation when one hosts a group, along with a hot meal and in some cases, overnight lodging in homes of church members. I have found that most people are glad to get to know the guests and to share their homes and food with them.

With regard to career music evangelists, keep in mind that "a workman *is* worthy of his hire," and many who are in full-time evangelism must set monetary minimums in order to live and be able to travel to their places of respective ministries. It is disconcerting, however, to see a few give "black eyes" to many by overpricing themselves. It is in these instances that we often see performances instead of ministries. Take care in selecting your guest artists. The ministry of music in your church can be affected for years by one instance of guest musicians who sought to exalt self instead of Christ.

Choir Festivals

It is good to encourage your choir or choirs to attend and participate in as many choral festivals as possible. Some of the good results are:

1. You hear new material that can be used in your church.
2. Your church group meets and hears choirs from other churches which can both encourage and inspire them.
3. When memorizing the music is required, choirs will leave with a sense of great accomplishment in meeting the challenge.
4. Comments from the judges, usually available on request, are of great value in learning about weak areas of the choir's presentation. Remember, this is not competition. Every choir that participates is a winner.

Choosing Who Sings Solos

In thinking about who should sing in church worship services, I try to be extremely careful about using the same people or ensembles too often. It is marvelous to have a good solo voice or voices in the choir. Blessed is the director who enjoys one good, strong solo voice in each section who can help carry that section. However, for one moment, put yourself in the place of the "nonsoloist." Some feel extremely inferior and are so afraid of singing a solo part that much coaxing is necessary to get them to even try. Being constantly overlooked and living in the shadow of a better singer two seats to the left certainly doesn't improve the ego problem.

One of the most regrettable memories I have is that of a man who sang in my choir for over five years. Never once was he interested in a solo part—or that is what I gathered—for he would shy away from even the suggestion. Yet, I never insisted that he try.

At a social gathering, during a visit after I had left that church and city for another position, many of the former choir members and my family gathered together to sing. When we started to sing one of the old favorites of the choir and came to the solo line, I suddenly heard a beautiful baritone voice that I had never heard before. Looking around, I was startled to see Bill, singing with a smile as big as all outdoors.

My first thought was that I had really missed out on a lot by not using him years ago! But, what I ended up thinking was, "How many blessings have I cheated this church of by not using Bill while I was here!" Look and listen carefully to your people. They can surprise you sometimes.

Financial Considerations

One other thing to consider, which is very important to any ministry in any church, is how much money is available to finance the music ministry. Find this out early in your ministry. It could be one of the most difficult areas of your entire ministry. Many churches look upon the music minister as a "miracle worker." They fail to realize that the "lovely choir number" on Sunday morning had to be purchased in quantity at an ever-increasing price. They expect only "the best," but find it hard to comprehend that a music minister will need to buy "several" selections per year for the choir. The out-of-tune piano creates immediate irritation, and the music minister gets instant reports of its "sounding terrible"—but "must we tune it *twice* a year?" (The answer is, "Of course you should!")

You, your pastor and the chief financial officer of the church should sit down together and discuss openly your plans and dreams for your ministry. Try to be as open and truthful as you possibly can be. Do not hedge on approximate costs and needs.

I recommend that you work up an actual music budget, which I believe is the ideal solution to seeing to the needs of the church music program. Try to allow for inflated costs over last year's quoted prices, even at the risk of the budget's being higher and supposedly harder to have approved by the church. Otherwise some purchases will have to be postponed because you have not allowed for price increases. Most of the time financial officials and ministers will share your hopes and goals, and usually take care of your needs. Remember, however, that there is a difference between fulfilling needs and fulfilling desires!

Should you find yourself without the needed monies, for whatever the reasons, do the best you can with what you have. Don't give up! My belief is if the Lord placed you there in your position, you can rest assured that he is as interested as you in seeing his ministry through music flourish. I have often been surprised at how many persons, having been touched by the ministry, will offer to help, with money as well as with needed leadership assistance.*

The Good News for You

You are in an enviable position!

Just ask that choral director who regularly directs his or her 100-voice choir on television. Ask him to be truthful! I believe he or she will join me and others all over the world in telling you that some of the happiest, most productive days of our ministries were in smaller churches with choral groups of limited size and ability. Not that we are not thankful for our present places of service. We know, however, that had we never been fortunate enough to serve in small churches, we would have missed a great part of our lives. We would never have learned vital aspects of our ministries had we not served with dear loving Christians in those churches. Our lives are richer for having shared in a ministry with them.

And, may you be so blessed!

About the Contributor: *Mack M. Moore has led workshops for Baptist part-time ministers of music and is especially sensitive and in touch with being in a small church setting, although he himself is a full-time minister of music.*

He holds a B.A. degree in Pre-law from Baylor University and the University of Texas. After being accepted to law school, Mack decided instead to study for a B.S. in Education, which he received from North Texas State University.

Beginning with music as his hobby, Mack has now become a full-time minister of music and has written articles for the Baptist Sunday School Board on the subject of youth music. He has been minister of music at Two Rivers Baptist Church in Nashville, Tennessee, Edwards Road Baptist Church in Greenville, South Carolina, and is presently at Glenview Baptist Church in Fort Worth, Texas. Mack and his family live in Fort Worth.

---

* Chapter 3 has some ideas about how you might raise money.

Nuts, Bolts and New Ideas

John Purifoy

5.

Developing Good Repertoire and a Balanced Choral Library

***From the editor:** Developing a music library takes thought, planning, money, time, and lots of searching. Developing an overall direction for your library is an important foundation which can lead to better choices and more economical ones as well.*

John Purifoy has written some of his ideas about this task, and I think you'll find some helpful guidelines around which to structure a well-balanced choral library—as well as some new ways to get more mileage out of your choir music dollar.

Director of Publications for Word Music, John constantly deals with having a well-balanced catalog within the range of Word's interests. He leads workshops, edits, composes, directs a staff of other editors, coordinates publication schedules, works with composers on potential publications, and keeps in touch with the variety of styles.

Often when I am leading reading sessions at a workshop or reading mail at my office, I have come across questions from ministers of music concerning musical styles, tastes and how to balance them. Some of the people are classically trained musicians who serve in churches which prefer gospel or contemporary styles. Others are somewhat frustrated about the ability levels of their choir, though they feel fortunate to direct people who love to sing and are eager to learn. It seems that one of the key areas of a music minister's responsibility is that of developing good "repertoire," or choral selections which will comprise music in worship.

I greatly enjoy participating in choral music, and I presently, have a part-time involvement as associate director of the college choir at my church. During the years of thinking about literature, I have come to hold some criteria important in developing good repertoire within a church music program. These pages will include some of those criteria.

To begin with, let me say that I will use the term "good repertoire" to mean music which is purposeful, workable, and meaningful for your unique situation. I will not deal with "good" and "bad" specific literature, because that involves decisions of taste which you will make along with others in your church. Therefore, I hope to give some guidelines which you can use to heighten your awareness, discretion and most of all "sensitivity" to the musical needs within your church environment.

There are four groups of people who influence and are influenced by the music used in worship: the singers (choir), the listeners (congregation), staff personnel (worship planners), and yourself, the director. All are equally important and represent one body of participants who communicate and receive musical worship.

Consider the Choir

Of these four, I will start with how I think the choir should be considered and involved in developing repertoire. First of all, the level of musical ability of the choir will be an ever-present consideration in choosing music. As you become familiar with this level, you will probably begin to sense a definite "parameter" within which you can select repertoire. At times you will want to stretch this parameter to challenge their abilities so that they can grow. At other times, you may want to aim for safe limits of difficulty so that they will feel effective and fulfilled both musically and spiritually. No matter what their level of ability, any choir can sing quality repertoire in worship if the music you have chosen fits their abilities and needs.

If the choir members' musical training as a whole is not as far along as you might like, do not be discouraged. Many publishers are aware of this need and offer a wide variety of creative, well-written choral arrangements of all styles for such groups. Many unison and two-part arangements have been written by able composers, offering high levels of musical value with workable vocal and keyboard settings. Also any choir can benefit from unison singing, including the large choir with a higher level of training. Singing in unison can be a great opportunity to improve blend, intonation and vocal quality within the ensemble.

In addition to the ability of the choir, it is necessary to take stock of their needs and tastes both musically and lyrically. It is understandable that many singers will not respond with excitement and commitment to music which does not appeal to them. Perhaps with time, certain styles will begin to have appeal, but try not to let your personal tastes always override what you know to be the needs and tastes of your singers.

One suggestion might be to have certain members of the choir, perhaps a music committee, take an active part in the music selection process so that you get a good representation of all tastes involved. However, be careful. There are good and bad representations of all musical styles, including classical, gospel, folk or contemporary.

While I was a graduate music theory student at the University of Texas, we evaluated programs for beginning freshmen music students. We examined a comprehensive analysis of literature from various styles and time periods. We were given listening assignments to evaluate from samples of plainsong to Renaissance, Baroque, Classical and Romantic period selections. Also included were selections in jazz, bluegrass, country, popular, rock and ethnic music.

After completing all listening assignments, to our surprise we were required to list qualities that "all" selections had in "common"! It was amazing to see how many basic common threads ran through such a diverse group of musical styles and periods! As a result of the assignment I had a more enlightened, well-rounded perspective of effective music encompassing all styles, current and past.

The same can be true, to a smaller extent, in church music. Choral directors of sacred music today are faced with countless styles of music from which to choose for children, youth and adult choirs. The same director is probably faced with as many needs and wants within the choirs as he or she is with available choral music in print. As long as he or she uses discretion in all areas, a good variety of musical styles (classical, gospel, folk and popular) can be extremely healthy for any choir program, and will probably include something for everyone. I have seen the Christian message communicated effectively in practically every style of music available. So it's up to you to discern what is effective and meaningful within your setting.

Consider the Listeners

Now, the second group: those who listen to the music you choose. This is the area probably given the least consideration by most choral directors, yet in Christian music, or any music that proclaims a message, it is of vital importance.

As a member of the church, you can pick up "by osmosis" likes and dislikes for certain music by members of the congregation (although I'm not saying that we should *always* try to conform to every suggestion we may receive!). Your ultimate aim should be for the congregation to comprehend messages through music in worship. They are on the receiving end of your communication through music, and if they are not "in tune," so to speak, with what you have chosen, it is unlikely that they will receive a message at all. So being aware of their likes and dislikes can help enable you to get the message across. To elaborate on an earlier suggestion, it might be wise to include non-choir members on a committee of some type which could evaluate the music and give input from time to time.

And if, by chance, you feel a great need or challenge to uplift and improve the musical standards of your church, it is best to try to do it gradually. A good method is to offer pieces they would like to hear combined with selections you feel will elevate the overall program.

Consider the Rest of the Church Staff

The third group, the church staff, is also a vital part of the whole picture. As the minister in charge of music, it will be as important for you to communicate to the other minister(s) what your goals and purposes are, as it will be for you to solicit their help.

A good procedure might be to let them know the thoughts and beliefs which motivate you and what results you hope to achieve through the music program. Then ask for their input and try to include some of their ideas so that they have an active part in achieving these purposes and goals. By trying to be sensitive to their spiritual and educational insight you can help create unity among the members of the staff, and music will become an integral part of worship planning. Also, this can help fine-tune your own spiritual growth as minister of music.

When it comes to working with the staff, particularly the pastor, you will probably be asked to choose music which coincides with a sermon topic or worship theme. I strongly urge you to choose pieces which are appropriate in *both* lyrics *and* music.

Many times I have seen a piece chosen because it contains a very appropriate lyric and message, but whose musical content has "failed on all, or most counts." In trying to achieve coordination, once a matching text was found, the search stopped.

It is important to try to avoid this natural tendency to by-pass your knowledge of musical workability and meaningfulness just to find the correct text. While this makes your search for repertoire much harder, taking the time to choose good music as well as text increases the effectiveness of you and the choir tremendously!

Consider Yourself

What then of your own personal visions and goals, now that I've mentioned my ideas on the other three components to be considered? To me, the ideal approach would be to try to constantly maintain a balance between what you personally know to be relevant to the people and therefore effective, and what you want to achieve in their appreciation of good repertoire. Try to be the steering force which channels various kinds of music leading in one central direction that ministers in all four areas by proclaiming the message of God's love.

The Balanced Music Library

A music library should include variety and balance—in the areas of voicing (SATB, SAB, 2-part, Unison) as well as in style. The choir probably fluctuates in size during certain times of the year, so you will need this variety for them. Also, at times adult choirs enjoy a taste of something with a "lighter" style and can be refreshed by it. On the other hand, youth choirs enjoy the challenge and "grown up" feeling of some rather sophisticated literature from time to time.

Where to Find New Music

With these basic ideas in mind, where does one go to find this balanced selection of music? One of the most consistent and inexpensive resources are publisher's preview plans. They are usually offered on a subscription basis, and the cost of the plan is often far less than the music you actually receive. A thorough plan offers cassette recordings of the music, rehearsal tips and aids, copies of new publications, and other benefits related to church choral music.

Although it might be overwhelming to belong to preview plans from *all* publishers, it would be a good idea to enlist with the publishers you feel have the most to offer your unique needs. Let your schedule be your guide as to how many plans you join. It will take time, interest and energy on your part to thoroughly evaluate all of the music that will cross your desk.

Another source which can be of great value is choral workshops. Sponsored by publishers, denominational associations, and music dealers, these workshops and reading sessions allow you to hear new music performed and give you the opportunity to read through music yourself along with other directors, thereby making evaluation much fuller and easier. Also featured often are seminars on various topics which are helpful to you as well as your accompanist.

Workshops are times of rich fellowship, sharing and learning among church musicians who hold common goals and have common needs. It's a good idea, therefore, to find out about workshops sponsored in your local area, and plan in your music budget for the financial means to be able to attend one or two a year.

Good music dealers who specialize in choral music can also be very helpful in your search for new available music. They have access to catalogs from various publishers and can give you advice or knowledge about what is new.

I must put in a comment here, however, about using your discretion when browsing at workshops, in preview plans or at music stores. Just because a publisher has deemed a work worthy of publication doesn't always mean it is worth performing. Unfortunately there are many works appearing in print that may not even approach your standards of musicality and meaningfulness. This is why it is of utmost importance to try to always consider lyrics *and* music as an entity, as what may appear to be a good text may be in an awkward setting musically (or vice versa).

Another category of church music which is often overlooked in repertoire search is that of choral collections not in the "norm" of most ten- or twelve-title compilations, such as books of service music, choral anthologies, compilations aimed at specific areas of need (i.e., seasonal, liturgical, and so on). These types of publications can help your music library become highly usable throughout the entire church year.

Non-Choral Music

In areas other than choir music, you are probably called upon for recommendations for soloists, instrumentalists, organ selections and informal sing-along occasions or Sunday school assemblies. Many times I have gone to well-compiled hymnals or sing-along collections in cases such as this. These books can also be of great value to the choir, because of the wealth of songs in many styles rarely found in one choral collection.*

If you have a flair for improvisation, there are many creative things that can happen with a book of this type (i.e., modulations, interludes, choral improvisations). These are excellent ideas for those last-minute special preparations, and the choir members will be given a rather out-of-the-ordinary challenge.

Timing the Search

One of the biggest "emergencies" we hear about at publishing companies is that of timing the search for seasonal music, particularly Christmas and Easter. There is probably more music budget money spent on long distance telephone calls and air mail postage due to this problem than anyone would believe. I recommend that you plan far enough ahead so that (1) you have enough time to make a sound decision, (2) there is a comfortable time frame to plan in accordance with the church calendar, and most importantly, (3) you and the choir have time to thoroughly learn the piece.

I recommend May, June and July for selecting and ordering Christmas music. In this way, your music should arrive by September at the latest for beginning rehearsals. By the same token, October and November are the best times to plan Easter music so you can begin rehearsals in January.

The Art of Maintaining Repertoire

I cannot end this chapter without putting in a word about what I call "the art of maintaining repertoire" with your singers. People come and go in the choir, and the number of members who sing on a given Sunday can also fluctuate. Therefore, it will be very important for the choir to maintain the knowledge of certain musical works which are worth repeating. When you rehearse

* The "Sing 'N' Celebrate" series are excellent for this type of use.

them, stress the importance of memory—not only of the music itself, but of interpretation as well, so you don't have to spend a great deal of time re-working the same pieces. By this I don't necessarily mean having the choir "memorize" a piece (though there are many directors who do require this on certain selections), but to be familiar with what a well-rehearsed performance should include.

The repertoire in your choral library can be the key to an effective church music program, and it requires your attention in almost every working day of your career. The potential of reaching the world through Christian music is great, and the effects of well-planned literature are unlimited. Imagine a set of balance scales with you holding the center. On one side lies *quality, creativity, meaningfulness* and *innovation.* Evenly balanced on the other side is *workability, appropriateness, effectiveness* and *need.* By sensitively developing a well chosen repertoire you can create this type of balance and your library will serve the purpose of greatly enriching all those who are touched by music in worship.

About the Contributor: *John Purifoy graduated from the University of Arkansas with a B.M. degree. He has also done post-graduate work in music theory at the University of Texas, where he held the position of Coach Accompanist, and was part-time choir director at Hyde Park Baptist Church in Austin, Texas.*

Some of John's compositions include such octavos as "Here Am I, Send Me," "Come to Me, All Who Labor," "Someday My Lord Will Come," and a Christmas cantata entitled A Son Is Given.

When there is time to relax, John likes to snow ski with his wife, Vicki, and spend time playing with his two young sons.

Richard D. Dinwiddie

6.

Planning the Worship Service

From the editor: *One of the aspects of worship that can often be slighted is the part done behind the scenes by the worship leaders, you and your pastor—the planning. A well thought out yet flexible order of service which takes the people comfortably into their own personal worship is a delicate thing to create. There are probably as many orders of worship as there are churches, some satisfactory, some stale and others vital and alive. What makes the difference?*

Richard D. Dinwiddie in a close relationship with Dr. Warren Wiersbe, refined some principles which helped the two ministers blend together various elements of worship at Moody Church of Chicago, and these principles are discussed in this chapter.

I first met Dr. Warren Wiersbe in 1971, when he became senior minister at Moody Church in Chicago. I had joined the staff as pastor in charge of music the preceding year. Dr. Wiersbe and I spent much time together, discussing our concept of the meaning and order of worship. Both of us believed that together, as the minister of the pulpit and the minister of the choir loft, we were co-ministers of the Word, each supporting and complementing the work of the other, both of us working more effectively than we could if we operated in "splendid isolation" from each other.*

* Dr. Lloyd Ogilvie discusses the relationship between the pastor and the minister of music from the pastor's point of view in Chapter 16.

Although the Holy Spirit often coordinates independent efforts, we did not presume that he would always do so. Throughout the Bible, God combines the principles of divine guidance and human preparation. God does not place a spiritual premium on lack of preparedness. We believed that each of us should know what the other was planning, both on a weekly basis and for the future.

Consequently, we met each Monday to review the preceding day's ministry, to plan the following week's services, and to keep each other informed about our long-range objectives. We also met frequently at other times. We found that through such mutual preparation and communication, we could accomplish far more than we ever could separately.

When planning the worship services, we would try to make all the parts of the service fit together to enhance and enrich everything that was said, sung, and done. We believed that this kind of service had the best potential for two-way communication between God and the individual believer, for worshiping him, learning about him, and finally making a spiritual commitment to him. However, we also tried to remember that order alone does not guarantee that genuine worship will take place, for it is possible to plan an order of service without worship ever really happening, or to have a poorly planned service and still experience the presence and power of God.

It seems it should be obvious that the primary purpose of a worship service is *worship*. Yet, in too many services, I have seen all kinds of activities, good as they may be, become substitutes for worship, thereby obscuring the basic purpose of the service. We cannot "create" a worship experience, only God can do that, but we can plan an order of service in which we create the maximum possibility for a well-rounded worship experience. John Robert Paterson Sclater said, "The purpose of the worship service cannot be fulfilled unless every member knows what he is doing and why he is doing it; and all this is impossible without an order." *

The Old Testament system of worship was highly organized, a system which David said he received from the Lord, together with the plans for the temple (1 Chron. 28:19). In the New Testament, when speaking of services of worship, the apostle Paul emphasizes, "God is not the author of confusion" (1 Cor. 14:33),

---

* J. R. P. Sclater, *The Public Worship of God* (Grand Rapids: Baker Book House, 1970 reprint of 1927), p. 17.

and "let everything be done decently and in an orderly manner" (1 Cor. 14:40, NIV). When we come together to worship God, our service of worship should be as thoroughly organized and carefully carried out as possible. God is a God of infinite detail.

The basic elements in a worship service are: praise and adoration, conviction and confession, teaching and communication, thanksgiving and sacrifice, and commitment. God sets this forth in two biblical orders of worship, one in Isaiah 6:1–9 (contemplation, conviction, confession, cleansing, calling, commitment and commissioning), and the other in 1 Thessalonians 5:16–24 (adoration, prayer, thanksgiving and edification, benediction and blessing).*

Basic Considerations

I cannot overemphasize my conviction that the minister of music is a minister first and a musician second. The purpose of ministry is not primarily to make music; the purpose of music is to minister to God and to the people. It seems to me that many church musicians lack an adequate concern about these priorities. This does not mean that the priority of ministry diminishes our musical responsibility. Since we serve the Creator of the art, we should be more highly motivated to do our best than those who serve only the art itself. We discipline our talent in order to serve God more effectively.

Even more than the discipline of musical talent, I believe that both being a serious student of the Scriptures and being familiar with the basic principles of scriptural interpretation are necessary to fulfill the requirement of ministry for a minister of music. In other words, if I am to responsibly minister the Word to our people and effectively coordinate my ministry with that of the senior minister, I must know what the Bible teaches and what position my church takes on issues where sincere people may have honest differences of opinion.

If we are to fulfill our responsibility to proclaim scriptural truth, then we must be careful about what we sing. If I am not familiar with theology, I cannot be adequately sensitive to theological problems in music. As a minister of the Word, I am as fully respon-

---

* For a fuller description of these orders of worship, see "Worship: Service or Circus" in my book, *Church Music Today and Tomorrow: Excellence in Theology and Practice* (Scottsdale: Good Life Publishers, scheduled to be released in 1982).

sible for verifying the theology of what we sing as is the preacher for the theology of what he says. It is tragic to me that so much of the music used in our churches is theologically inappropriate.

Content must precede style. As a diamond is more important than its setting, however beautiful that setting may be, correct theology is more important than good music, no matter how beautiful it is. Beautiful music is not an acceptable excuse for singing wrong theology.

Therefore, I feel it is important to read through every hymn to determine whether or not you agree with the theology of each stanza, and note ahead of time which stanzas of a hymn are to be deleted. If the text of the hymn is not in agreement with your interpretation of Scripture, it should not be used, regardless of how popular that particular song might be. If we do not take the theology of our music seriously, we should not be surprised if ministers do not treat our music as seriously as we think they should.

In planning the music for the service, one needs to know the scripture text and sermon topic as well as the response the minister wants from the people. Dr. Wiersbe always tried to let me know his plans in advance. (Sometimes, leaders in a service act as if the Holy Spirit does not know what he is going to do until he does it!) Study the text. Pray over the text and try to understand its main points clearly. If there are questions about the meaning or how the text will be interpreted, talk with the minister about it.

All of the music used in a service need not be directly related to the message. In fact, a service with only one theme could be the exception, not the rule. Therefore, there usually is variety in the musical content of the service. The average congregation is a group of people with different individual tastes and preferences. They come to the service with varying experiences and expectations. While one selection may stir someone's heart, a totally different type of selection will meet the need of another person. Try to select music that will minister to a cross-section of the people.

There are times, however, when you might prefer similarity to contrast in order to emphasize a particular point. In such a service, all or most of the musical selections may be on the same theme. In making choices, take into account the total music of the service—choral, solo, congregational, and instrumental. A contrast of style and mood may be desired, or, on certain occasions, a similarity of style and content may be preferred. Whether the music is similar or contrasting, try to achieve the variety of basic objectives in the worship service, as stated earlier.

What should the people do as a result of the music? Try to plan music with a precise answer to that question. Every selection in the service must have a definite purpose or set of purposes, such as praise, teaching what we believe, sharing our faith, giving thanks, or responding to God. Too often, hymns are selected merely because the people know them well and, therefore, will sing them with relative confidence.

Selecting the Hymns

Once you have a grasp of the sermon and the desired response from the people, and using what you know about the Bible, the interpretation of it and the hymn texts, I suggest selecting the hymns for the congregation, beginning with the closing hymn. The final hymn seems to be the most difficult one of all to select. The singing of this hymn is usually the moment at which each person is asked to make a personal response to the total ministry of the preceding hour. Many times the final hymn can move minds and hearts to respond to the message which has been presented.

Unfortunately, I have often found that no selection in the hymnal really relates to the theme of the message. In such cases, I try to select a hymn which is of a general nature of commitment, thereby giving the pastor maximum flexibility in asking for a response to his message.

The first hymn in a worship service should be a *hymn of praise to God.* As much as possible, the text should be objective, emphasizing the character, person, and attributes of God, without major emphasis on what he has done for us. I believe God wants us to praise him for himself.

If there are three hymns in the service, the middle hymn can be from a wide range of categories. It may be a setting of Scripture (as may also the first hymn), a hymn on the topic of the sermon, an expression of witness, or another hymn of praise. I try to plan every hymn so that it has a specific spiritual function to fulfill, *never* merely to "fill time," "stretch," "open windows," or move people around. To use a hymn "to do something by" is to train people to ignore the real meaning of what they are singing. If any of these movements are necessary, and if we prefer to have music to mask the noise, ask the organist to play something vague, without obvious religious content.

Sometimes music leaders and pastors hesitate to use something unfamiliar, even if it has a great text which matches the message almost exactly, for fear the people will not sing "enthusiastically." At the same time, however, it is generally unwise to choose all unfamiliar hymns for any given service. People need to have some sense of security in their music. If there are three congregational selections in a service, see that at least one of them is a familiar one. Also keep track of when hymns are sung, using as many as possible, so that you do not use only a few select favorites, ignoring many of the great treasures in the hymnal. I have often had students tell me they thought their home churches, by continually singing the same few hymns, rarely including anything new or unfamiliar, had deprived them of a hymnic heritage which they felt was rightfully theirs.

Resist the temptation to hurry through this selection process, and always take great care to choose the best possible hymns for a particular service, even though this may take a great deal of time. I have often spent several hours in restudying the hymns, trying to select those which I think correlate best, if at all, with the message. The average topical index at the back of most hymnals is only a starting point. Some hymnals now include an index to scriptural allusions in the hymns, which can be quite helpful. However, there is no substitute for really knowing Scripture and hymnody. Even the best indices are incomplete and often erroneous. Study the hymns in the hymnal, making sure that the pastor and you agree on the choices made for the services.

Unfortunately, in many churches, the musician is not sufficiently acquainted with the hymnal to make the wisest selections. In many instances the pastor is more knowledgeable than the musician in matters of hymnody. In such cases, the pastor is better equipped to choose the hymns for the services.

Once you have chosen the hymns, tell the pastor what you have decided, particularly the closing hymn. Or give him a list of recommendations to choose from, depending on what emphasis he prefers. At times, there are good reasons for even changing the closing hymn from what is printed in the bulletin; for example, the message may develop somewhat differently than originally planned. Both you and the pastor should be sensitive to this possibility.

Selecting the Music for the Choir and Soloists

Choose the music of the choir and soloists as carefully as the hymns. There are occasions when the music should relate directly to the sermon, especially if any excellent musical setting of the sermon text is available. Of course, this can best be done when you are given enough lead time to rehearse such choral or solo selections.

It is very helpful to know what anthems in the choral library are based on scriptural passages. Since these are not always identified on the published anthem, have an index prepared which indicates all the scriptural allusions in the choral texts. It takes time to set up the index initially, but the result is well worth it.* It is important to keep the index regularly up-to-date as new selections are added to the choir library.

As with the hymn choices, however, plan contrasting types of musical styles. For example, if there are two vocal/choral selections in the service, it is good to have one accompanied, the other without accompaniment; or, one may be objective, the other subjective. One may be a great anthem, the other a setting of a familiar hymn.

The impact of the choral anthem can often be strengthened by printing the words in the bulletin. No matter how clearly the choir sings the words, if the people can also read the text, it helps them to focus their attention on the meaning of the text. After all, since the point of using the music is to communicate the message in that song, the music has little value in the service if the text does not get through to people. When people can see the words while they listen to them being sung, they have a better chance of understanding the text. What they see reinforces what they hear. Also, if they take their bulletin home, the message of the music continues after the service itself is over. (It is important to request permission from the copyright owner to print the text, and then to follow their instructions about putting the necessary copyright notice and other information in the bulletin.)

The choral call to worship should be just that, a call to the individual to step *now* into the presence of God. Since even the most beautiful and meaningful call to worship becomes common

---

* Chapter 4 includes a description of a good filing system for your music library.

after many hearings, teach several different ones to the choir so that there is a variety from which to choose. Likewise, have several choices for a choral benediction.

Selecting the Instrumental Music

I have frequently observed that the instrumental service music is often irrelevant to the service, having very little to do with the various acts of worship taking place. The prelude should be a time when each worshiper prepares himself or herself to commune with God. All too often, the people in the congregation pay little or no attention to the prelude. As far as I know, it is not possible to prepare one's heart for worship while enthusiastically talking to the friend in the next seat about children, golf scores, recipes, or football games. It is little wonder that when this has gone on during the prelude, a worshiper still seems to need several minutes after the service has started to "get into" what is happening.

To help worshipers prepare themselves during the prelude, we found it helpful to insert the following note in the bulletin: "At the first note of the organ, let us bow quietly in prayer, and prepare ourselves for worship." Regular reminders from the pulpit can also be helpful, even necessary.

The offertory is when some of the greatest musical sins are committed. First, it is very difficult for people to concentrate on anything being sung when they have to fuss with wallets and purses and are distracted by ushers walking around in the aisles. Therefore, I rarely plan a choral offertory selection.

Second, often the instrumental music chosen for an offertory bears little or no relation to the act of giving. This part of the service is not an "intermission" or a "recital" time for the organist, but, rather, a moment when we offer ourselves to God; and the portion we place in the offering plate is a symbol of our giving our whole selves. The offertory should reinforce the meaning of the offering. If the selection has a familiar text associated with it, the text should remind the listeners of words of consecration, committal, and so on. The mood may be contemplative, or it may emphasize the idea that "God loves a cheerful giver" (2 Cor. 9:7).

Ideally the postlude should convey the basic or concluding mood of the service. If the service has been very introspective, this is not the time for the Widor *Toccata.* On the other hand, if the service has been one of grandeur in praise, the Widor might be very appropriate. So often, "service music" is selected on the basis of what the organist wants to play, for whatever reason, rather than what would contribute the most spiritually to the service. Organists can be made aware of your feelings in these areas and learn to be sensitive to them in selecting music for the service. Let the organist know the theme and mood of each service in time to make appropriate choices.

Nonmusical Worship Elements

One of the problems in planning a service is the ever-annoying announcements. Frequently, they are grouped with the offering. This can subtly distract from the meaning of the offering because the service comes to a dead stop at the announcements and has to be started up all over again, making it almost impossible to have a steadily moving "flow."

One purpose of the bulletin is to note the necessary announcements. If the bulletin is read aloud to the people every week, they are subtly conditioned to ignore it. Even so, there is always the possibility that some important announcement has been left out, or needs special emphasis, or that something significant has happened since the bulletin was printed. One solution which, to us, had fewer drawbacks than most is to place the announcements *before* the call to worship, so that the service can move steadily onward from the call to worship to the benediction without interruption. If announcements *must* be made, I think this is the "least bad" place to put them.

Another distraction is caused by latecomers hurrying to their seats after the service has begun. Latecomers should be seated only at selected points in the service, to minimize this distraction as much as possible. A note to this effect can be placed at appropriate places in the printed order of service. The ushers are given the responsibility of seeing to it that seating of latecomers takes place only at the designated times. The organist should be asked to play quietly at these points.

In the pacing of the service, try to avoid lengthy pauses so that you can keep a sense of "flow." The principle of inertia applies to services, too. Try to avoid breaking the order down into a series of individual events, marked off by an endless chain of awkward starts and stops. Yet, at the same time, try not to race through the service. Each event has its own meaning and dignity. I have found that this sense of significance can be preserved by setting certain events next to moments of meditation as the organist plays discreetly.*

The Pastor and You

Henry Ward Beecher, the famous preacher of the Plymouth Church in Boston, once observed that "music is the worship part of the service; the sermon is the instruction part." ** The pastor and music director must plan carefully together and understand each other's role if this fusion of ministries is actually to occur. An effective worship service cannot be planned in half an hour. It takes time to study Scripture and music, pray for guidance and insight, select repertoire and coordinate your plan. It also takes time to work together. Be willing to spend that time to achieve the goal of a well-planned worship service.

I recommend a frequent review of your own services as well as occasional services in other churches, in case there is anything that can be done to increase the effectiveness of your ministry and worship. Since we serve a God who commands our worship (John 4:23, 24), we must do all we can to make our corporate worship as glorifying to God and as meaningful to his people as possible.

About the Contributor: *The Rev. Richard Dinwiddie has done doctoral studies at Case Western Reserve University, holds an M.M. from Cleveland Institute of Music, and a B.A. degree with majors in organ and English from Kent State University. He has studied privately under Robert Shaw.*

He has taught church music, hymnology, music history and conducting at Case Western Reserve University, the Cleveland Institute of Music, and Trinity College in Deerfield, Illinois. He was Director of the Sacred Music Department at Moody Bible Institute, where he also conducted the Moody Chorale. He served as the pastor in charge of music at Moody Church from 1970 to 1980, and is presently director of choirs at First Presbyterian Church, Deerfield, Illinois.

Richard has written articles for Moody Monthly *and for* Chris-

---

* A sample order of service from Moody Church is included at the end of this chapter.

** Henry Ward Beecher, *Yale Lectures on Preaching* (New York: Fords, Howard & Hulburt, 1881), pp. 144–145.

tianity Today, *where he is contributing editor in music. He also wrote a performance guide for an Easter cantata by Claude Bass,* We Have Seen the Lord, *published by Word. He recorded the album* The Lord Whom We Love *with the Moody Choir for Word Records. He is an active leader in church music conferences and clinics throughout the United States, as well as conducting concerts. He is currently writing books on conducting and church music, including an anthology of letters written to his choirs and a book on music and worship being co-authored with Warren Wiersbe.*

Some of Richard's other interests include photography, magic, philately (collecting postage stamps), model railroads, books and listening to music. He and his wife, Ruth, live in Chicago.

Sample Moody Church Order of Service

June 17, 1979

At the first note of the organ, let us bow quietly in prayer, and prepare ourselves for worship.

10:50 A.M. MORNING WORSHIP

Organ Prelude: "Morning Has Broken" —Trad. Gaelic, arr. Fasig
*Welcome, Registration, and Announcements
*Organ Meditation
Call to Worship
Choral Praise: "Let Heavenly Music Fill This Place" —G. Young
Doxology
*Hymn No. 19 "Ye Servants of God" —William Croft
Scripture John 18:1–11
*Organ Meditation
Choir: "Jesus, the Very Thought of Thee" —Dale Wood

Jesus, the very thought of Thee with sweetness fills my breast; but sweeter far Thy face to see, and in Thy presence rest. / Nor voice can sing, nor heart can frame, nor mem'ry find a sweeter sound than Thy blest Name, O Savior of mankind. / O hope of ev'ry contrite heart, O joy of all the meek, to those who fall, how kind Thou art, how good to those who seek! / But what to those who find? Ah, this nor tongue nor pen can show; the love of Jesus, what it is, none but His loved ones know. / Jesus, our only joy be Thou, as Thou our prize wilt be; Jesus, be Thou our glory now, and through eternity. (Text: attributed to Bernard of Clairvaux)

Pastoral Prayer
*Organ Meditation
Offering
Offertory: "Son of God, Eternal Savior" —Dutch melody
Dedication of Babies
*Hymn No. 10A "When This Passing World Is Done" —Richard Redhead
Choir: "Surely He Hath Borne Our Griefs" —Karl H. Graun

Surely, surely He hath borne our griefs and carried our sorrows. (Text: Isaiah 53:4)

MESSAGE: "Kisses, Swords, and Cups"
Dr. Warren W. Wiersbe

Hymn No. 481 "So Send I You" —John W. Peterson
Prayer of Benediction
Choral Benediction: "Closing Prayer" —Ron Harris
Organ Postlude: "Joyful, Joyful, We Adore Thee" —Ludwig van Beethoven

(William Fasig playing the service; Diane Mesner, piano)

* Latecomers will be seated

12:00–12:45 P.M. Visitors' Reception, with light refreshments served; in Kappeler Hall (downstairs).

Aubrey Edwards

7.

An Orchestra in Your Church—You Can Do It!

***From the editor:** Perhaps in your secret dreams you've imagined yourself conducting a breath-taking, inspiring performance of a large choral work accompanied by a full orchestra. Or maybe you've been restless lately about your music program, looking for a way to expand it, liven it up, include more musicians. Or your oldest daughter just won a seat in the school band playing flute and you're looking for a way that she can use this talent at church as well as at school.*

Wherever the spark of interest comes from, the actual job of putting together an instrumental ensemble can seem enormous, especially if you've not yet had much experience with this kind of music or musicians since college or seminary days.

Aubrey Edwards has served in four churches as a full-time minister of music and has started an orchestra in the last three churches. By now he has established a procedure which can lead to enrichment in your own music program and which is easy to follow.

For many years choral music has been the main thrust of a minister of music's energies. Maybe an occasional instrumental solo is included, but not much emphasis has been placed on creating ensembles and orchestras which would meet together regularly and take on a responsible role as a part of the church's music program.

But something which excites me very much has happened to church music during the last ten or fifteen years. We've become more and more aware that God created instruments which we can use during worship and which provide a colorful and interesting variety of sounds. Job's reference to the timbrel and the lyre (Job 21:12) and David's use of the harp to accompany his psalms, as well as the classic sacred choral works by Bach, Beethoven, Brahms, Handel and others which were performed with orchestra all indicate that instrumental music is pleasing to God and enhances worship by his people.

Some time in 1965 as I sat at my desk in the music office thinking about all of this, I decided to start using more instruments in the worship services and concerts of my church in Nashville, Tennessee. "Even if we don't experience the 200,000 silver trumpets Josephus said were used in the great Temple of Solomon," I thought, "we can certainly begin to sing hymns accompanied by a brass choir, or even a solo trumpet!" *

During the years that followed in that church and in the two churches I've been in since, I found that it is quite possible to develop instrumental music programs out of congregations with little previous experience, and it has added a new dimension and depth to my ministry in ways I couldn't have imagined. I noticed a renewed enthusiasm for my work at the church that I hadn't felt in months as I began with excitement (and a little nervousness) the process of learning what needed to be done to fulfill the dream of having an orchestra in our sanctuary one day. And I have noticed that when people become involved in this program at the church, as the orchestra members have done, often their relationship to God deepens, as well as their commitment to the church.

At first my brain fairly flew with lots of questions and few answers: Will the pastor and the rest of the staff approve and cooperate? What ways can I use instruments? What will it cost? How can I find out who plays an instrument in the congregation? Where do I find out about conducting, union players and so on? Where will we rehearse?

Will the Pastor Cooperate?

Before I approached the pastor at my church with this idea, I tried to put together as much of the information about why

* Josephus, *Josephus, Complete Works,* trans. by William Whiston (Grand Rapids: Kregel Publications, 1960).

and how we could develop an instrumental program as possible. When we met, I started my presentation with the reasons I felt it would enhance our worship services as well as involve more people. I gave some specific examples of how I might use the instrumentalists, and some "ball park" figures of the cost. I then laid out a plan for finding players which included three ingredients I feel are important: prayer, visitation and use of the music committee. (More details about these will follow.)

By being prepared, I hoped to show my willingness to commit time and energy, plus by belief that the program was worth beginning. His enthusiasm and support were invaluable to me later and I was glad I had talked with him early in the game plan.

How Can Instrumentalists Fit into Worship Services?

It soon became apparent that a group of instruments can add a completely new dimension to the music in a worship service. Here are a few ways I have tried using the players in the worship services.

One of the basic uses of instruments is to accompany a hymn, which gives support to the congregational singing. Also, I involve players in the worship services by having a soloist, a trumpet trio or some other small ensemble play the special music. Featuring a group or a soloist fifteen minutes prior to a service is a wonderful way to prepare the congregation for worship.

Sometimes I use a solo instrument or full group from the balcony. A group in this position has also accompanied an antiphonal choir. However, I've found that only after a group has played together for awhile, can they advance to playing with a choir.

It is exciting to include instrumental groups at seasonal times like Christmas, Easter and Thanksgiving. It seems so appropriate to enhance the seasons which highlight the key reasons for our faith. Fortunately there is more literature available for these seasons than for the general church year.

Another seasonal occasion is the Fourth of July weekend. I have found that it becomes an exciting opportunity to exalt the relationship between God and country by planning special services. When others are thinking of firecrackers, I am thinking of how I can use brass, drums and other instruments in a worship service of patriotism and praise to God for our country.

When a group has had enough experience together so that there is a good balance and enough repertoire learned, they can present an instrumental music program for a special occasion, or during part of an evening worship service. But try to be sure the group is ready so that it is a positive experience for the players as well as the listeners.

Ensemble Combinations

Here are some instrumental combinations which work well together:

Basic Brass	*Combination*
3 Trumpets 2 Trombones French Horn Baritone Tuba	Basic Brass Plus: 2 Flutes 1 Oboe 2 Clarinets
Contemporary	*Full*
Combination Plus: String or Electric Bass Guitar Drum Set	Contemporary Plus: 5 Violins 4 Violi 2 Celli (This is what I use for 40–60 singers. I adjust this number up or down according to the number of singers.)

What Will It Cost?

The equipment I began with and the approximate minimal costs are listed below:

Instrumental Folders (Some local music stores have complimentary folders they give for publicity.)	$1.50–$2.00 each
Music Stands (Sometimes players have stands at home they will bring to rehearsal until you can acquire enough stands for all.)	$15.00 each

Music costs for the year might be something like this:

Published orchestra parts or orchestrated hymnbooks (3 sets)	$150.00
Full scores to be used with choir	$ 80.00
Manuscript paper for making your own arrangements	$ 30.00

This is similar to the beginning budget with which I started. Items can be added slowly as needed when the instrumental music program begins to grow.

How Do I Tell Who Plays an Instrument?

Sitting in a worship service on Sunday morning, I looked out over the faces in the congregation. *How do I tell the instrumental players from the rest of them?* I wondered. I devised a plan which I later learned is not the best way to enlist players. An announcement in the church paper invited all those who played an instrument to come for a rehearsal. When the rehearsal night came, four drummers, five saxophone players and one trumpet player showed up! Although I appreciated their interest, the result was less than I had hoped.

Even though I was a little discouraged, I kept thinking. Finally I came up with an idea which has proven to be one of the best ways I have found to uncover the musical talent in my church. I asked the minister of education to help me take a survey throughout the Sunday school (ninth grade and above) on a certain Sunday. Here is a sample survey card which we used in our survey:

INSTRUMENTAL MUSIC SURVEY

Name ____________________ Phone __________
Address ______________________________
Sunday School Department ____________________

( ) I cannot play any type of musical instrument.
( ) I can play a musical instrument. Give name of instrument. ____________________

How long have you played this instrument? __________ (years)

In addition to this survey, I visited the local school band directors in Nashville who gave me more information about who plays and how well they play. In most cases, I found them very helpful and glad that the students might have an opportunity to get more experience playing their instrument.

Using the information I secured from the survey, I began personally visiting the players to ask them to join the orchestra. In this way I got a better variety of instruments, and I could explain more about what the plans were and also answer any of their questions.

It was a great temptation for me to invite just those who had played for a good number of years and had the instrument under control, but I made an effort to include players at all levels when I could.

In trying to decide who would play the first chair parts, I set up an audition for each member. The audition included (1) playing a scale, (2) playing a hymn from the hymnal, transposing the melody at sight to the proper key for the instrument being auditioned, (3) sight reading their part from a typical hymn arrangement for instruments, (4) interviewing them to find out if they were going to work in the program and also what their "spirit" was. This key person is very important, because in the first chair position he or she will be able to pull the others through many difficulties.

Using Professional Musicians

I try in every way to involve people within the congregation in the instrumental group, but sometimes I need to go outside the church to hire additional musicians. It may be that a particular instrument is needed and I can't find anyone who plays it, or that I need to enlarge a section for a particular performance. I rely on three main sources: the local bands, the youth orchestra and the civic orchestra. People from any of these groups should be paid for their services.

Local band directors can recommend students; then I talk to the student directly about the specific project for which I want to hire him or her. I usually ask the band director in advance what the going rate is for the students. I assure the student at the very beginning what the payment will be, when it will be paid, and I try always to honor these commitments. It can cause hard feelings if you fail to mention payment or change it to a lower rate after the performance. I figure the payment based on the number of rehearsals they attend, and sometimes if a student has to drive an unusually long distance for rehearsals or performance, I add a little extra for this.

In all three towns I have been in, there has been a youth orchestra whose players I hire from time to time. I followed the same procedures for hiring these young people.

When hiring players from the civic orchestra, you will be hiring members of the local musicians' union, which means that every musician hired who belongs earns a set fee established by the union. Here are a few suggestions based on my learning experiences with professional musicians.

Find out about the union rates by calling the symphony orchestra office. There is a person at the office who can give the rates or refer you to someone who knows.

Whenever you need members from a musicians' union, the first thing to do is hire a contractor whose responsibility it is to select and hire the players requested, have them at rehearsal and performances promptly, and take care of paying them. The contractor usually gets a double fee for this service. This is the traditional way of working with union players, and it is a valuable service, saving hours of telephone calls and administrative red tape. You also have to issue only one check for the total amount, and the contractor takes care of each individual payment. The symphony office can give you the names of several contractors if you don't know any. If you have a friend in the symphony who knows the contractors, you can get good references this way.

The contractor has a contract which he or she asks you to sign. Make sure, before signing, that you know what is in the contract. Take time to read it thoroughly, even the fine print. Space does not allow pointing out all the aspects of a union contract, but one thing to think about before the performance is whether or not it is going to be recorded. If it is, you need to get permission from each union member before recording. This is a union requirement.

When working with union players, be very careful to start and stop rehearsals *promptly*. This is a business precaution, since the union players are hired for a specific time, which has been told them in advance. At the end of that time the player is entitled to get up and leave the rehearsal, even if you are in the middle of a passage, so try very hard to finish within the amount of time stated. After some experience, you will be able to give a fairly accurate estimate of the time needed to finish a rehearsal.

It is also good discipline for the nonprofessional and student members of the orchestra. Remind them not to delay the beginning of a rehearsal, a policy I try to enforce whether or not there are any union players involved. One effective way to get started is to stand up and give a signal for tuning to the principal violinist exactly on the dot of the hour the rehearsal is to begin. Union players are accustomed to this and will be ready to play, and this will usually send any stragglers scurrying to their places.

You should know about the Musicians' Trust Fund in New York City (a national organization). This fund will pay 50 percent of the cost for union musicians in rehearsal and performance, if your performance is for public enjoyment, is nonprofit and if you do not take an offering or charge any admission fee. When you request these funds, you will be required to send in half the cost before the first rehearsal. You can probably find out the rest of the details about how to enjoy this fund through the local symphony office or union office.

Finding Music for an Instrumental Group

I'm always searching for arrangements to meet the needs of my church instrumental players, and I have found that there is only a limited amount of material available. I started my search by asking many publishers for up-to-date catalogs of all published instrumental materials. Sometimes there are sample recordings of the arrangements which I purchase. This is especially true of choral collections or musicals with published instrumental parts. In some cases publishers rent instrumental parts for a particular work; however, most of the time the arrangements must be purchased. Check around with other churches who have instrumental groups. It might be that you could rent, borrow or purchase a used set of instrumental parts.

Since it is very expensive for a publisher to print orchestra parts, and the demand for them is lower than for choral music, usually only a small quantity of a select number of titles are printed. As the demand for instrumental music increases with the beginning of more and more church instrumental programs, the amount of music available will increase. From time to time, write to publishers letting them know of your interests and needs.

Sometimes the printed parts are written for professional "recording studio" musicians so they might be beyond the ability of the players in your church. I study each part before selecting anything for the group, and try to become familiar with the capabilities of the players. It is sometimes possible, with a few revisions, to use most of the parts, but I watch especially for difficult runs and wide ranges. Try not to embarrass or discourage the players with music beyond their abilities.

Arranging for Instrumental Groups

It has happened more than once that I needed to write parts for a particular piece of music because I couldn't find a published arrangement of it. When I first began doing some arrangements,

I had to re-learn some facts about transposing and about the range for each instrument. I looked these matters up in Walter Piston's book called *Orchestration,* published by W. W. Norton. There are several other good music text books about orchestration which will serve just as well.

Before I tried any instrumental parts for a major work, I experimented with some simple writing, such as taking a hymn and writing parts for the instruments I had available. Using an instrumental writing chart which gives the range of each family of instruments, I tried my hand at writing and then let my players play the arrangement for me. I learned a lot by this trial-and-error process.

Here are a few specific suggestions:

1. Use the organ or piano to help the instrumental group by filling in missing parts, strengthening weak parts and helping keep the instruments in tune.

2. When there are more players than parts, double (in order of preference) (a) the bass an octave lower, (b) the alto, (c) the tenor, (d) the bass at the unison, (e) the soprano, (f) the soprano an octave higher.

3. All instruments whose orchestration key is C are nontransposing and, therefore, may play directly from a part on a piano, organ or vocal score, so long as it remains within the range. This saves copying time.

Sometimes I ask some of the players themselves to help, or find a professional arranger who does free-lance work. But I hire a pro only if the cost is already budgeted.

What Makes a Good Rehearsal Room?

The physical surroundings for the rehearsal are very important. The room should be large enough to give everyone room to sit and have sufficient space to play his or her instrument. Also, try to make sure the room has no posts or other obstructions to block the view of the conductor.

The chairs should be chosen to support the backs of the players. The Wenger music chairs (No. 100AK) are excellent because they have a straight back and padded seat which give good back support and comfort during the rehearsal. Also, you could use some nonfolding stackable chairs. My players tell me that the typical metal folding chair found in most churches is not comfortable for them because the back slants too much to support them properly.

It is preferable to have the instrumental rehearsal in a separate room from the choir room. There is a good deal of time-consuming work involved in setting up the chairs and music stands, and sometimes I have simultaneous but separate rehearsals with the choir and orchestra. A friend who is a band director and also in the congregation often rehearses the orchestra while I rehearse the choir up to the final rehearsals when we put them together.

If you aren't fortunate enough to have this qualified assistance, you might want to schedule the rehearsals on the same night but one right after the other. It helps to have the instrumental rehearsals in a separate room from the choral ones.

How Can I Best Contribute to the Orchestra? (Rehearsals and Conducting)

To me, an important key to any instrumental program is to try to be the best conductor you can, and be prepared. Before I have any rehearsals, I make sure I study the instrumental parts thoroughly. If there is a conductor's score, I mark it so I can easily give entrances, dynamic markings and releases. Colored pencils are my favorite method for this. After studying the score and marking it, I practice directing in front of a mirror until I am comfortable with all of the entrances and dynamic instructions.

To continue to improve myself, I try to take advantage of every chance to learn about directing and instrumental arranging. I keep reading, consulting with college music faculty, professional musicians within the congregation (like the band director and the symphony member), and attend workshops sponsored by publishers where instrumental choral works intended for church instrumental groups are performed.

Publicizing Performances

A congregation loves to be informed when "the big occasion" is scheduled, and the members of the instrumental group like the publicity, too. So I suggest putting an announcement in the church newsletter or the Sunday bulletin the week before saying that the instrumental ensemble is going to play. Remembering this small detail, I believe, helps the players feel the appreciation from the director and from the congregation in a much more concrete way.*

Resources

Here are a few books which are very useful resources:

Brand, Erik D. *Band Instrument Repairing Manual.* Elkhart, Indiana: Erik D. Brand, 1939.

Farkas, Philip. *The Art of Brass Playing.* Bloomington, Indiana: Wind Music, Inc., 1962.

Keenan, Kent. *The Technique of Orchestration.* New York: Prentice Hall, Inc., 1952.

Piston, Walter. *Orchestration.* New York: W. W. Norton and Company, Inc., 1955.

Posey, Phillip C. *Strings and Things: Building a Successful Instrumental Program.* Nashville: Convention Press, 1974.

One More Step

After three years of developing an instrumental program, I realized my present church in Birmingham needed and wanted an ongoing instrumental program that would continue to supply us with players and help those we already had to improve. We decided to go one more step and consider starting a music school.

After visiting churches who had instrumental music programs, I made notes about whatever their programs had that we might be able to begin in our church and collected these notes in a file. A committee was formed to study the practicalities of developing a music school; it included a person who had done community interest programs with the University of Alabama, a CPA, the children's choir coordinator, our organist, the band director and several members of the choir who were interested.

Next, we took a survey of the congregation to find out if there was any interest in having a music school. We found the interest level high. So we projected a budget and took it and the results of the survey to the finance committee and the deacons of the church.

These two groups approved our plans, so we began to solicit the faculty for our school. We placed ads on the bulletin boards of the schools of music at nearby universities, in the local paper

---

* More details about ways to promote concerts can be found in Chapter 15.

and in our state denominational paper. To everyone who responded to the ads we sent a "teacher application." Each person who returned the completed application was given an audition and an interview.

From this group of applicants we hired teachers and began registration for the students, and on January 13, 1980, six months after we surveyed the congregation, our music school was born, with plans to start a string program in the fall. Our school opened with thirteen faculty members and 105 students. We offer both classes (in guitar and voice) and private lessons (in piano, voice, trumpet, trombone, French horn, flute, percussion and guitar). I am involved as administrator to help keep it all going, plus I benefit from the new instrumental players being trained.

In all the lessons we give at the school and in the group rehearsals, we try to instill in each person what we believe is the reason for playing. We believe that even if we have attracted the best of talent and have provided outstanding musical leadership, but have forgotten that it is all done to glorify the Lord and show his love, it will become as "sounding brass or a tinkling cymbal."

About the Contributor: *Aubrey Edwards holds a B.M. degree from Samford University and an M.C.M. degree from Southwestern Baptist Theological Seminary. He first went to Temple Baptist Church in Newport News, Virginia. After three years he moved to Belmont Heights Baptist Church in Nashville, Tennessee, where he developed a recording youth group, and a television ministry, as well as his first orchestra.*

Next he became music director at First Baptist Church in Hendersonville, N. C., where he developed another orchestra, conducted concerts for the governor and took his choir to Washington, D. C., to sing on the capitol steps. He also helped establish mission churches through the music program.

Aubrey is now minister of music and youth at Shades Mountain Baptist Church in Birmingham, Alabama. He performs major musical works with orchestra and choir, and has produced a dramatization of The Messiah *with a cast of 250. He conducted premieres of "The Witness" and "Here Comes the Son" with a 100-voice youth choir, and his adult choir sang the second World Premiere of Kurt Kaiser's musical, "Just for You," at a Word-sponsored music workshop in Birmingham in 1979.*

David Stuart Blackburn

8.

The Impact of Small Ensembles in Your Music Program

***From the editor:** How many times have you enthusiastically started a new women's trio, men's gospel quartet or youth contemporary group only to have it fizzle and die after the "new" wears off? A few experiences like that could be enough to convince one that ensembles are just too much trouble to worry about. Of all the elements that combine to give a small ensemble life, there seems to be one key ingredient. This can keep ensembles alive and make them not only long lasting, but an intimate shelter in which deep spiritual growth can take place.*

"Let the word of Christ dwell in you richly in all wisdom; teaching and admonishing one another in psalms and hymns and spiritual songs, singing with grace in your hearts to the Lord" (Col. 3:16).

The writer of this letter to the Colossians believed as I do that music can be a dominant force in shaping human life. Good music can be used in a church setting to praise, honor and glorify God. It can strengthen and nurture our faith as it provides a potent vehicle for corporate worship.

I also believe that music is one of the most important and powerful means to communicate God's love. I clearly hear a call from God to find more ways to use that power. I feel the need to search constantly for creative new ways to provide for the fullest flowering of a vital and effective ministry through music.

Some of these questions I continually ask myself and would ask you in these pages are: Am I effectively developing all of the musical resources of the church? Am I aware of the talents of the members of the congregation? Am I sensitively and creatively ministering to the musical needs and preferences of all groups in our congregation? Out of my own attempts to answer these questions has come the discovery of the impact, breadth and greater depths of ministry which can come through small vocal ensembles.

Why Bother with Small Ensembles?

In my opinion, small vocal groups are a vital part of a well developed music program. When I began to establish such groups in a church, I felt fearful at first. But I also felt called somehow to reach beyond the traditional notion that "church music" meant one general choir for each age group. I remember having to overcome my own reluctance to make the effort to "disturb" the congregation, which I felt had a complacent attitude. I wanted to challenge them to more personal growth and discipleship through more involvement in music activities. It would be much safer, I realized, just to drift with the traditional past. The congregation would probably never know the difference if I continued being content to lead a children's choir or two, develop a youth choir around the promise of a special trip, and an adult choir that pleased the congregation every Sunday.

But to my delight, I have found that people enjoy participating in small ensembles. And I have seen many kinds of benefits—benefits to individuals, to the choir itself, to the congregation as a whole and even to the entire community. And these benefits helped me see that having one or several small ensembles does not weaken, but strengthens the entire body.

Benefits to Individuals

One positive effect is that small ensembles, once developed, may act as an attraction to people in the church who were not involved with the choir. The smaller group's flexibility in rehearsal times and places, and the emphasis on his or her musical interests are what often appeal to such people. This involvement many times leads to involvement in more of the total music program.

Since small ensembles are less cumbersome and more personal than the whole choir, I have found that they are a better place for people to develop their particular area of personal enjoyment and satisfaction. People have told me that they feel deeper fulfillment singing music in which they are personally interested. And an important insight for me was to see that when someone in the church has a chance to develop the talents God has given him or her, this often seems more meaningful to each person than many other outlets for these talents outside the church.

Benefits to the Choir

Even though there seems to be a variety of different voice types, personalities and musical tastes within most choirs, I believe that the choir as a whole should try to present a balance of musical styles and try to blend those various differences into a smooth, well-balanced program.

Recently in a nearby church, a group of choir members told the music committee that they wanted more classical music to sing. Another group, when they heard about this, complained in the other direction and added that they represented the musical taste of the congregation as well! Meanwhile, the choir director was trying to keep a balance and variety in the music repertoire.

If I had been in that choir director's place, I might have done something like this. I would carefully think it over to make sure I was truly balancing the variety of styles. If I saw I was not, I would make a renewed commitment to the choir to improve the balance and give classical music its rightful place in that balance. But either way, I would also talk to them about my philosophy for the choir, my belief that they could all benefit from singing a wide variety of musical styles if they would try to have an open attitude. Also, I would tell them that I felt their ministry was to the congregation, which has a mixture of musical tastes. After having said all this, I would respond directly to the specific unhappy choir members with the offer to form small vocal ensembles specializing in the musical style they preferred—classical, gospel, or whatever.

A second benefit to the total choir is the possibility for musical improvement. Each singer in a small ensemble is more exposed, with fewer people on which to lean. So his or her skills develop faster. This individual improvement in sight reading, ear training, balance and blend brings a noticeable benefit to the larger choir.

Benefits to the Congregation

With the many musical styles of today and the many preferences held by members of the congregation, having several small ensembles is the best way I have seen to satisfy those various preferences. The ensembles help provide a better balance and more variety, which helps avoid the tendency to expect the adult choir to sing mostly traditional anthems and the youth choir to sing music with a more contemporary style.

Benefits to the Community

Outreach is another benefit. And to me this is a vital factor and key reason to develop small ensembles. Beyond the individual, the choir and the congregation, the ensemble can have a ministry to the community. Service organizations and civic clubs are always looking for good entertainment, which gives ensembles from the church a chance not only to entertain but also to tell others about their lives as Christians. Performing outside the church also gives a way to help bridge ecumenical gaps through cooperating in special services and weekday programs with other churches.

Types of Ensembles

There are many types of small ensembles to consider when starting a program. One type is a small chamber or madrigal group which can perform music like that of the Italian Renaissance (music by Orlando di Lasso, Palestrina and Gabrieli, 1450–1650) and early Baroque periods (Schein, Scheidt, Schutz). Another source of music for this group is from the early English period of sacred choral music (William Byrd, Thomas Tallis, Christopher Tye are a few of the more well-known composers from this period). A striking effect can be achieved if this type of group can be accompanied by a harpsichord and a cello playing the continuo part. If there is a consort of musical instruments of this period available at a local college or university, their use can greatly enhance the performance. Sometimes recorder choirs are used to complement the small madrigal or chamber ensemble. One possible highlight is to have a Christmas madrigal dinner served by the singers. Wearing appropriate costume, they also present the entertainment, which includes early carols.

A second possibility is a small ensemble which could begin with a few voices as a double quartet (eight singers, two on each part) to perform traditional and gospel hymns. There is a rich heritage of early hymn texts and tunes which comes to us from Germany and England. And it is exciting to re-discover the uniqueness and beauty of the early American hymns and folk tunes.

Also, a ladies' and/or men's ensemble can provide an added dimension. There are pieces written or arranged for such ensembles which give much greater expression to the text and nuance of the music than that of the mixed choral sound.

There is a growing interest in smaller ensembles which perform "contemporary" gospel and sacred music. So much music is being written and widely accepted in this style that there is plenty of room to have more than one group of this type. Each one can have its own unique musical style and delivery. Ensembles can range in size from small (three to six voices), to medium (six to twelve voices) to large (twelve to twenty voices). Each group seems to form its own personality, whether it is built around one or two individuals or a blend of the whole with accompanying instruments.

One important factor in this type ensemble is to have the proper microphones, speakers and other sound equipment for the singers, in order to produce the appropriate style and blend. Equally important is the back-up instrumental group which usually consists of one electric lead guitar, bass guitar, drums, piano or electric piano, and perhaps an organ or synthesizers. The electronic effects from the singers' sound system combined with the instruments become very important in getting the right contemporary sound. I have found that this type of ensemble is particularly popular and effective with youth groups and younger adults.

It is also fun to form groups that perform secular music and scenes from musical comedy for sheer recreation. It is healthy, it seems to me, for the church to provide such an outlet. It provides a lot of fun for the participants, while allowing them to bring enjoyment to many functions of the church and especially the community.*

How to Get Started

These are just a few possibilities to start your mind working on your own situation. The first reason for developing small ensembles for the church, I believe, should be spiritual. The second is musical, as a means of developing skills and providing variety in the music program. But in my experience with small vocal

---

* See Chapter 12 for more details about music with drama, and Chapter 10 for more details about organizing a major performance.

groups, it is only when hearts are united in the spirit of God's love and power that he can be glorified, which is again the ultimate purpose.

It seems easier to encourage participation in small ensembles if time is taken to get to know the choir and to know the congregation and the kinds of music they like. It is best to start with one ensemble at a time, adding others when the time and leadership become available. This allows time to build quality into each vocal ensemble, which is one of the best ways I know to attract people. I have developed some guidelines which I try to follow in starting new ensembles. These are written below with the hope that they may be helpful to you in beginning a program.

Try to make it an honor to be in one of the small ensembles and carefully select the members with emphasis on how well they "fit" into the ensemble for which they are chosen.

To start the first ensemble, select a few of the talented musicians who seem to have spiritual depth and personal commitment. Then seek to provide both spiritual and musical leadership yourself. It is so vital for the whole ensemble to begin to participate in sharing and spiritual fellowship with each other within the group. I have noticed that this forms not only a blend of their spirits, but also of their voices.

Start with a meeting which combines singing with a short devotional. Share your philosophy of spiritual fellowship and hopes for this kind of fellowship to develop among the members. Also begin to pray together. I lead the prayers each time, but provide quiet space for other members of the group to pray aloud if they want to. Emphasize that the spiritual and musical go hand in hand, and one cannot function without the other in achieving the purpose of ministry.

I have known small religious groups that have formed, putting on the "Christian smile" while performing, yet in real life having no fellowship or spiritual depth. This kind of musical experience, although it may be pleasant at first, is usually shallow and in my experience does not last.

When that first ensemble develops with a spiritual base along with careful guidance as to style, blend and interpretation, then you can call on those experienced members to help start other ensembles. By asking people from the first group to be directors or influential leaders in other ensembles, you can be more assured of the continuation of both spiritual and musical growth. To me it is best if the original group can continue to be a supporting spiritual center for each individual to "come home" to as he or she goes out to the new ensemble.

Choosing the Singers for Each Ensemble

In most cases, it is my feeling that formal auditions are not necessary in the church. Different styles of ensembles can be developed throughout the church as well as different levels of difficulty, thus providing a chance for all who want to participate. I try constantly to keep watch as a director of music lest I begin to "play god" in telling people who can and cannot participate. I have found over the years that there is a place for almost everyone. And I believe it is important for us as ministers of music to try to find the right place where people can be most effective and happy. Most of the time through the normal routine of rehearsals it is easy to tell who is regular at rehearsals and worship services and who would be willing to accept this extra responsibility.

When I am not familiar with a certain voice, however, I sometimes ask the person to sing some scales so I can find out his or her best range. Also I might request that he or she sing a song in the style of the ensemble.

Choosing the Music

Music that is right for a particular ensemble is very important to the success of the group. For me the first criterion is whether the text is meaningful and theologically suitable. Then I consider whether the music conveys the text in the best way to reach my congregation. And, of course, the musical style should match the style the particular ensemble has chosen to sing.

With as many music companies as there are today publishing music for all ages and in various musical styles, it is important for directors to attend church music workshops and reading sessions sponsored by music publishing companies to get a chance to go through a lot of material efficiently and to be better able to select music which can minister to each director's choirs and congregation. Keeping fresh music which will challenge the ensembles and speak to the congregation is a never-ending process which is nevertheless of great importance.*

---

* See Chapter 5 for more about where to find suitable music.

Naming the Group

Many times the name of an ensemble is as important as a person's name. The name identifies both the personality and the purpose of the ensemble. The Bible is full of words and phrases, like "The Second Chapter of Acts," "Regeneration," "Bridge," "Morning Star," and "Agape."

When an entire group participates in study, discussion and prayer about their name, there seems to be a new bond which develops among the members. The bond is created by a sense of purpose or meaning shared and understood by each member. Choosing a name is a process which helps create unity within the group.

Choosing What to Wear

Along with the name, the choice of clothes worn by the members helps project the personality of the group. Whether formal or informal, there are many different ways to achieve unity through dress. If all the girls or women are to wear one style and color of outfit, and the boys or men another coordinated outfit, try to keep in mind that it is important to find clothes which are both proper and complimentary to all types of people. For example, what looks good on a smaller person might not look as attractive on a large person. There are styles which are suitable for all. Another way to present a unified, though not rigid appearance is to choose common colors for all, then allow each person to put together an outfit which is different and pleasing to the individual, yet still complements the whole ensemble.

I believe that great emphasis should be given to how the ensemble looks, because sharing the love of Christ through song with a congregation is not only audible, but visible. Sometimes the way a small ensemble looks can detract and distract from their ministry to the congregation. I cannot overemphasize the importance of keeping that aspect of ministry before us at all times. Our choice of music, our dress and our actions can add or detract substantially as we try to bring glory to God and minister to the congregation.

The Right Blend: Vocally, Spiritually, Personally

Although every choir member need not join a small ensemble, each ensemble offers a necessary extension and outlet for many people who have the interest and the musical ability. I repeat that I think it is important to select people who blend well together vocally, spiritually, and personally. At times I have seen the wrong mix of people. Just one or two who do not seem to fit or who cannot seem to adjust to the group can destroy the entire ensemble. Sometimes at this point difficult changes have to be made for the good of the whole ensemble and for the individuals themselves.

I believe that we as ministers of music should be the ones to create the first few small ensembles as well as to be involved in them musically and spiritually. I know that the process means a lot of extra work and maybe even headaches and problems, but this is the risk of being in ministry. To me the end results have merited any sacrifices involved.

About the Contributor: *David Stuart Blackburn has spent a lot of time working with small ensembles. David is a college music professor and part-time minister of music. He holds a B.M. degree from Westminster Choir College, an M.M. degree from Indiana University and a D.M.A. degree from the University of Iowa. David teaches voice, choral conducting, choral literature, history of church music, choir organization and development, and diction. He has taught on the music faculties of Baylor University, McMurry College, and is presently Chairperson of the Church Music Education department at Scarritt College in Nashville, Tennessee.*

David has also served as minister of music at Audubon Forest United Methodist Church in Atlanta, Georgia, Polk Street United Methodist Church in Amarillo, Texas, Austin Avenue Methodist Church in Waco, Texas, and St. Paul's United Methodist Church in Abilene, Texas. Several of his anthems have been published by the Chorister's Guild.

Kurt Kaiser

9.

Revitalizing Your Choir Rehearsal

From the editor: *One area of communication which can be very critical is that which exists between you and the choir in rehearsal. Often it seems that you can hear in your mind what the music should sound like, but sometimes it's quite a challenge to get this across to volunteer singers.*

Kurt Kaiser has worked with the world's top professionals and with some wonderful volunteer choirs. He communicates well. I have seen him spend forty-five minutes working on the phrasing of a three-measure line and have a group of volunteers sounding like professionals. And yet, for a while, Kurt wasn't sure he could explain on paper exactly how this process happens. It evidently doesn't happen the way we expect, with words and paragraphs. It seems to be an experience and an attitude in which one participates.

This chapter captures Kurt's ideas in a challenging approach which I think can give you new insights about communicating with choirs.

One of the first things I did after completing the formal study of music was put the *Harvard Dictionary of Music* on a shelf in the corner because time is precious! I have found that there is very little value in using technical theoretical terminology when working with untrained volunteer singers. Certainly theory ought to be learned, proper breathing, proper vocal techniques and hymnology ought to be studied, but not during the choir rehearsal time.

The "average" choir member, in my opinion, is not interested in vocal pedagogy: he or she is in the choir because of a love for singing and a feeling of definite commitment to the music program and to the Lord. But choirs are comprised of homemakers, secretaries, dental assistants, doctors, lawyers, school teachers, auto mechanics, and so on. They have come to your choir rehearsal to sing.

Through the years I have observed the rehearsal techniques of some astute conductors. I recall observing Robert Shaw, presently the conductor of the Atlanta Symphony, at work with nonprofessional singers. He demonstrated vocally, emotionally, and by descriptive stories, how he wanted a passage of music to sound. Before finishing his stories the choir could hardly wait to sing for him. And how they sang!

Dr. Thor Johnson, past conductor of the Cincinnati Symphony, and director of the Moravian Festival, was also in charge of the orchestra program at Northwestern University while I was a student. I loved to watch him work. He sang phrases to demonstrate the shading he wanted.

Sir Georg Solti, the conductor of the Chicago Symphony Orchestra, also sang phrasing, accents, and rhythmic passages in rehearsals. Even the very subtlest nuances can be achieved this way. It was obvious to me that these men knew the music thoroughly, but they conveyed their wishes with a noticeable absence of Italian or German music vocabulary.

One other person who has been a great help to me, and who always seems to achieve an amazing degree of musicality with large choirs in a short period of time, is Ralph Carmichael. First of all Ralph has instant rapport with volunteer choirs. I realized how important it was to get the chorus working *for* you—not *against* you. I noticed also how much fun the rehearsals were with him in charge. When things got tense, he would lighten up the atmosphere with a story, relax the group and then they would get back to work. He taught me a great deal.

A few years ago I was involved in a recording session in Chicago. Numerous members of the Chicago Symphony were hired to play. After the session was over, I asked one of the players to tell me who, in his years of playing with the Chicago Symphony, was the one conductor who got more music from the players than any other conductor. I expected him to say Sir Thomas Beecham, Eric Leinsdorf, Solti, Zubin Mehta or Leonard Bernstein. He told me I would be surprised by his answer—and I was. He said, "Kurt, the one man who got more music out of us than anyone else was . . . Danny Kaye! He has such expressive eyes. Ninety percent of conducting is done with the eyes." That's a most important thing to note in working with large choirs. Cliff Barrows has expressive eyes, and his eyes convey what the music says. Choirs respond to your eyes.

One of the important prerequisites is having music in which the musical lines are easily sung. That does not imply that the music is simple, but it does mean that the music is free of difficult intervals, augmented fourths, and so on. It seems helpful to give careful attention to this factor when selecting music for a large chorus when you have a short rehearsal time. This is true of any volunteer choir for that matter.

Several months ago a tremendous group of 1,000 voices from numerous churches across the state of Oklahoma was assembled. There was also a fifty-piece orchestra. I had this "gang" for a one-hour rehearsal. They had been sent the music and were prepared—some more, some less! I decided that we would sing through it one time, and then I would give a bit of background about the circumstances out of which the music came—why I wrote it, my intentions for it, the emotions I felt, where the "music" was to be found, where the climaxes were, and so on. Next we took apart whatever rhythmic problems there were and then put it all back together. We made it work! And I sensed that it was rewarding for everyone as they became involved in the music and sang amazingly well.

Taking the time to describe whatever the subject of a particular passage is—the anguish of the crucifixion, the glory of the resurrection, a sunrise, a storm—and then have the choir sing it, is a rewarding experience for me as well as the singers.

To get a large chorus to truly sing pianissimo is difficult to do, and some directors won't try—they settle for mezzo-forte all too soon! For me, when a chorus finally does sing with a delicate soft tone, a luxurious sound results. Part of the problem is to get choirs to listen. One technique I have used which helps choirs learn to hear one another works well with any size group. I start them singing very softly, then have them walk quietly around in the room intermingling sopranos with basses, sopranos with tenors, altos with basses and altos with tenors and so on, all the while continuing to sing softly. After they begin listening to each other, I work at getting a uniformity of the vowel sounds. Also, final consonants must be together.

In my work with choruses I usually spend little time having them vocalize. So often, I have watched choirs go through warm-up routines thoughtlessly which does little if any good. That time is better spent reading new music, in my opinion. There is, however, one vocal warm-up which immediately gets the members of the choir involved because they are forced to listen to one another.

Hum or sing "ooo," very softly, breathe whenever necessary, but keep the sound sustained. After I have assigned each part a specific note in a chord, I then instruct verbally and with a visual cue to have the sopranos move down one whole step, the basses up one half step, and so on. Here is an example of a chord progression you might use:

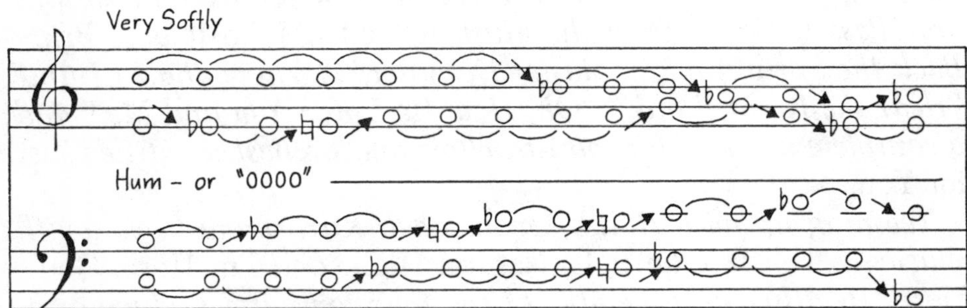

This exercise in listening and thinking while singing ought to be done without any assistance from a keyboard. Any series of half or whole steps will do. However, I feel it's best if the sequences are worked out in advance and come to logical resolutions.

I have always rehearsed as much as possible without the use of an accompanying instrument. Church choirs rely so heavily on a keyboard that it slows down the process of learning considerably. Take that "crutch" away, and though it will be tough going for a while, you will soon find that your group can sight read much more quickly without the keyboard.

Baylor University has an excellent football coach named Grant Teaff. Coach Teaff is also a committed Christian. I will never forget what he said about teamwork. His text was from 1 Corinthians 13, known as the "love chapter." "Love is a very powerful word," he said. "Husbands, you love your wife, and she knows it—but you have to *tell* her you love her. The same is true for you wives—tell your husband you love him, even though he knows you love him." Then he said a startling thing. He said, "I love my players, and my players love me. And I tell my players I love them. Now don't you think if I tell my players I love them, and they know I love them—they'll do anything I ask of them?" You see, that's what makes for teamwork. We need to exercise that kind of teamwork with our choirs by loving them. You will be astounded at how well they sing!

***About the Contributor:** Kurt Kaiser is Vice-President, Director of Music, for Word, Inc. He is involved in some phase of virtually every Word recording, as arranger, producer or conductor. He has also recorded several albums himself at the piano, and often gives piano concerts.*

In addition, Kurt has written hundreds of arrangements including songs for solo, choir and instruments. Among his compositions are "Pass It On," (from the Musical, Tell It Like It Is*), "Bring Back the Springtime," "Master Designer," "Where Shall I Run," "Hear the Right, Lord," "Oh, How He Loves You and Me," and a complete musical for soloists, choir and orchestra entitled* Just for You.

Teaming up with Ralph Carmichael, Kurt wrote three youth musicals: Tell It Like It Is, Natural High, *and* I'm Here, God's Here. *He also was a member of the four committees which compiled "Sing 'n' Celebrate," "Sing 'n' Celebrate II," "Sing 'n' Celebrate for Kids" and "Everybody Sing 'n' Celebrate."*

Kurt holds B.A. and M.M. degrees from Northwestern University and received an Honorary Doctorate of Sacred Music degree from Trinity College. He also enjoys playing handball and tennis, and traveling with his wife, Pat.

Will K. Andress

10.

The Choir Director As Producer

From the editor: *The stage is set, the audience hushed, the choir standing nervously in the wings waiting for the big entrance and the opening of the musical! How many times has this vision crept into your mind and sent secret chills down your spine? Only to be replaced by colder chills when you remember all the details it takes to get there!*

This chapter is about how an experienced director gets all those details into manageable form and makes events happen. Maybe you've tried a couple of productions already, and they went fairly well. But now it's time to polish. Here are pages full of ideas, methods and attitudes which might be the very thing you have been looking for.

Move over Cecil B. DeMille, here comes the choir director! Today there is a parallel between the producer of a Hollywood spectacular and the producer of large musical works in the church. This comparison is not necessarily related to the size of the audience, but more with respect to the amount of work involved in production, financing and effect.

There was for a time very little to compare in these two areas. Few churches ventured past the Sunday anthem, an occasional cantata, or an oratorio, the mainstays of American church music for many decades. However, the floodgate was opened twenty years ago when the youth musical phenomenon exploded upon us. To many, this seemed to be a new idea, but actually it was not.

Not too many centuries ago it was common to find the "First Church" of Florence, Paris, or Heidelberg presenting a musical drama to act out some great spiritual truth for people who could neither read nor write. They were painting that picture worth a thousand words. These "miracle plays" were very effective tools in the religious education and evangelism of the day.

Up until the late 1800s, the church had been the primary patron and supporter of the arts. Most of the great architecture, music, literature, and painting had been effected at the request of and with the financial support of the church. So we are not beginning in a new area, but are just returning to an old practice.

Here in the twentieth century, we find our people wanting and expecting much more than fifty-two anthems each year and cantatas at Christmas and Easter. They see and hear the finest musical dramas possible on television every week, and we choir directors are hard pressed to compete with the quality to which our people have become accustomed. Everyone, from elevator operator to bank president, has become a music critic. The critic in the newspaper is the least of our worries. Our concern is for the opinion of the one in the pew.

Seminaries and graduate schools have not, as yet, developed a course titled "Musical Extravaganza 101." Nor has "K Tel" or "Ronco" come out with their "Never-fail Producers Kit." There are, however, certain steps to follow in producing a large musical drama. These steps can ease us over the hurdles and help to insure success. There will always be the unforeseen, last minute problems, but these guidelines have proved beneficial for me and, I hope, will do so for you.

Whether deciding to present an oratorio, music concert, or a staged musical drama, the greatest decision to make is whether it is needed at all. Does it serve the purpose of the church, and in particular, our program? Doing for the sake of doing is not enough.

Most churches seek to justify their music programs in four areas; worship, education, outreach, and ministry. In other words, if I plan a choir tour, present an oratorio, stage *Godspell* or *Fiddler on the Roof,* have a children's choir camp, take my choir kids to sing at a nursing home, or add brass to the anthem on Sunday morning, will it be advancing the kingdom for my people in one of these four areas? This is a significant question.

Sacred and Nonsacred: Each Has a Place

Music and musical drama need not be on a religious or church subject, however, to be worthwhile as a church presentation. I think that there are many benefits to be derived from a quality Broadway styled musical if it can be considered to have a "G" rating. Although some Christians may disagree with this approach, the production of this type of program can provide wholesome entertainment for the audience—and for the choir. Many of our people have been brought back to church by these musicals after having participated in the community theater, a working environment that is not always appealing to Christians.

We can provide an outlet for this talent and at the same time bring people to the church for more of their "relaxation hours." This, it seems to me, is as worthwhile as sports teams, scouting, crafts, exercise classes, and the many other nonreligious programs which we have traditionally provided.

Another significant factor is that many so-called secular plays are able to drive home great universal truths about such things as integrity, love and the power of laying down one's life for others. Since I believe that all such truths are from God, it is my opinion that when *carefully chosen* and placed in context, such works can sometimes be used in unique and life-changing ways within the church.

An important thought to be raised pertains to the wholesomeness of the show. Will it embarrass the church? Will it foster an idea to which the church is opposed?

Many shows that are successful on Broadway usually require some editing for church use, and we do this without apology. Once this is done, you can have a fine experience producing it. Our production of *Pippen* required extensive re-working, *Oliver, L'il Abner, Jesus Christ, Superstar,* and *Annie Get Your Gun* only slightly. *Godspell* and *You're a Good Man, Charlie Brown* were left intact.

Choosing the Right Show

After determining that a musical is appropriate for a certain time in our program, the next task is the choice of the work. Questions begin to arise; will it fit the season? If I present this show now, can I have the choirs ready for Christmas, Easter, or the final program of the choir year? Will it interfere with our regular worship responsibilities? The organization of the entire program and year becomes very important, and I consider a musical production as only part of the entire picture.

I have drawn together a talented stage director and a choreographer, who along with the church organist and myself act as a board of directors for determining the productions and organizing the resources. Each person offers his or her own expertise and realm of contacts into the decision of the group. This team shares the responsibility as well as the credit for any good results. The first two persons mentioned have now become a part of our church membership as a result of this involvement.

In looking for the right show, one of the primary questions is, "Do we have the resources to stage the production?" The ingredients of lead performers, chorus, accompanists, and all of the technical workers needed are very important. To cast beyond our capabilities invites disaster.

For example, to plan to stage *Oliver* without a fine boy soprano, *Fiddler on the Roof* without a striking baritone with Jewish characteristics, *Oklahoma* without a great chorus, or *Jesus Christ, Superstar* without a strong rock tenor is out of the question. Building on what you have or can find is very important.

Also of primary consideration is a show's appeal to audience as well as performer. If the chosen piece is challenging and has appeal to the performers, I have found that rehearsal attendance holds up better, and this usually indicates that the show will be well accepted by the congregation and community. This, in turn, helps build a favorable reputation for the future. Attempts to force something on a congregation often lead to short tenures. So what we produce is important to our jobs as well as to the needs of the people.

Musicals that include children or have an element of comedy usually have a built-in formula for success. Almost all parents love to see their children on stage and may help recruit an audience. If the show has good music, looks good, is done well and makes people feel good about having come out to see it, you will have a hit. The first audiences may pass the word, increasing the crowds through the run of the show.

I discovered that our shows were beginning to bring larger and larger segments of the nonchurch community to our church. This was something that our planned evangelistic efforts were not able to do. Some of these people found their way back on Sunday. As a result, I commissioned a composer to write a Broadway styled musical with intended appeal to both the church and nonchurch people, titled *Go Out Singing.* The show, based on post-Easter experiences of Peter, has reached thousands so far.

Getting the Financial Picture

Financing a show is an equally strategic hurdle. The costs of costumes and staging usually increase proportionately with the size of cast, number of scene changes, period of the setting, and so on. Shows where fairly contemporary clothing can be utilized are much less costly, as the cast can usually find most of what they need in the attic or purchase it from secondhand stores.

A budget outlining expected income and expenses is a basic need at the beginning. We include on the "expense" side such items as performance rights, rentals and purchase of scores, promotion and printing, costumes, sets, props, and fees for instrumentalists and any professional assistance needed.

Next, on the "income" side, we list any budgeted finances available, friends who will help underwrite the costs, and ticket sales. I have served in churches where we tried to interest patrons by making a public announcement but did not get much response. When we made a one-to-one request, the result was often financial support.

We have also begun charging a modest ticket price with repeat performances and can now break even.

Ticket sales and finance constitute one area that should be given to a special finance committee. For me, preparing the show is job enough without the additional details required to build an audience and keep the books. Musicians (including me) are not known for their financial expertise.

Many musicals, as well as many other large choral/orchestral pieces, require the payment of a royalty fee to the person or organization holding the performance rights. This fee is usually required to be paid early in the preparation. Fees for performance rights are usually based on number of performances, size of auditorium, and admission charge. The publisher of the music can put you in contact with the person or organization holding the performance rights.

The rental of parts is based on the amount of time the materials are used. This is usually two months for vocal parts and one month for orchestral parts. A penalty is added if the parts are returned late or require extensive erasing of markings and notes. I try to be careful to ask my people to make their notes with a number two lead pencil and then erase those marks before returning the parts.*

Choosing the Right Performers

When the auditions are set, I allow at least five minutes per performer. I gather the stage and musical directors, rehearsal accompanist, and choreographer to reach a group decision about the right people for the show. Even though I may have thought of possible performers when choosing the show, I've found it is best not to "pre-cast" the show. Be objective! This is important in establishing trust that anyone has a chance for parts in future shows and auditions. And I've been surprised more than once during auditions by someone's outstanding ability.

Publicity in the Newspapers

The publicity committee should prepare a publicity release about the cast after they have been chosen and then follow up every week with an additional story. Look for any means to get a story in the paper.**

Newspapers can be called to come and take photographs when the costumes are ready and there is a set for background. The media is usually agreeable to using three or four different photos over a two-week period.

Most newspapers have a rule concerning repeated coverage. They usually will not run a story or photograph that has appeared earlier in a competitive paper. The committee will have to be careful in awarding the stories.

Choosing the Production Committee

Since there are many steps involved in the count-down toward performances, I usually need help with stage direction, sets, costumes, choreography, lights, sound, and so on. Almost all art disciplines are brought into the music drama, and most communities have sources of help readily available for the asking.

I have found high school drama, art, and music teachers anxious

---

* More details about where to get music for an orchestra, or how to start an orchestra can be found in Chapter 7.

** See Chapter 15 for more details about publicity.

to utilize their talents outside of the classroom. And they can often provide some labor force from among their students. The local college and community theaters have almost always proved willing to loan materials, lights, platforms, and costumes, and to advise, and even at times, provide labor. The smaller and more close-knit the community, the more likely this is to happen.

I have also called on local dance teachers and martial arts instructors for help with the physical movement of the people on stage. We have made use of Kung Fu students in recent productions when healthy, graceful male dancers were called for.

Dance instructors often recognize the value of having their names and their work before a different segment of the community, so they are willing in many cases to take part on a volunteer basis.

The house manager takes care of ushers, tickets, programs, time for opening the door, and so on, leaving me free to take care of other things. This person is the chairman of a committee that takes responsibility for everything that takes place on the audience side of the stage.

Setting the Schedule

When the performance date is set, I have found it a good practice to work backwards with respect to setting rehearsal dates and times. Likewise, while checking for performance conflicts, i.e., other in-house church programs, community concerts, the symphony, programs in other churches, holidays, and so on, I also check for conflicts with the last week or two of rehearsals. Everyone needs to be present for the polishing, especially if an orchestra is involved.

A printed rehearsal schedule is very important and helps prevent many misunderstandings. I publish mine and have it available at the auditions so all who try out for a part know at that time what the schedule will be.

Approximately three months of rehearsal time is usually needed for the presentation of an oratorio and six weeks of heavy rehearsals for a staged musical. This does not indicate the relative degree of difficulty of each, however, because choirs usually rehearse music without drama once each week, while musicals with choreography and/or drama are blocked and rehearsed nightly for a more compact span of time.

The staging director will usually make the rehearsal schedule by scenes so that we utilize the performers' time to best advantage. This rehearsing by scenes lets persons not involved stay home for the evening.

In preparation for *Annie Get Your Gun,* we scheduled a read-through by the entire company and followed it by rehearsals of the chorus and principals on alternating nights for two weeks. We then began to block and rehearse scenes for two weeks which still did not require everyone's involvement every evening.

The last two weeks were very demanding time-wise because of major rehearsals every night. These rehearsals were devoted to joining larger segments of the show until we were rehearsing by acts and, finally the entire show in costume.

The Dress Rehearsal

I like to invite an audience to the dress rehearsal because these people will give response to the performers so they can begin to adjust their timing for laughter and applause. Besides, I think that this is an excellent trial run for the novice as well as seasoned trouper.

There is an excitement about a dress rehearsal that can only be surpassed by opening night. Along with the flowing adrenalin comes the nagging thought, "Did I forget anything?" And it is better to have this thought the night *before* opening night!

Beginning for Yourself

I hope that you may be feeling by now that the staging of a musical is not the overwhelming challenge it might appear, if you assume the role of producer and rally a supporting staff. No one can do it all. I have included an outline at the end of this chapter which can be used as a basis for beginning your own planning.

For me, the reward for all of this effort comes when audiences are pleased that they attended, the performers ask what the next show will be, and show personnel begin to unite with my church. I usually become so excited that I actually want to start the process all over again!

After the dust has settled, but while details are fresh in my mind, I call a "recapitulation" session for my central committee. I usually have a few spots to cover and make plans for improvement. Sometimes the question even comes up about whether or not to stage another extravaganza. The remembrance of the good times in Christian fellowship during rehearsals, the development and use of God's gift of talent, the pleasure of the audience, and the sparkle in the eyes of the performers is enough, however, to dismiss a "whether" with a "which one and when!"

* * * * * * * * * * *

Production Schedule

I. Pre-rehearsal Planning
   A. Is there an appropriate place for a show and will it meet one of the purposes of music in the church?
   B. Organization of the key leadership to proceed further
   C. Factors in choosing the musical
      1. Will it have appeal for performers as well as audiences?
      2. Is the subject matter within the expectations and policies of the church?
      3. Do we have the performance forces required?
      4. Is the money available in our budget? Or can we get the money through other means?
   D. Set the dates
   E. Order the materials and pay the fees
   F. Hold auditions
   G. Complete the work force
      1. Technical director
      2. Costumes
      3. Lights
      4. Props
      5. Promotion and ticket sales
      6. House manager
   H. Prepare and post the audition schedule

II. In Rehearsal
   A. Rehearse to economize the work time of people
   B. Gradually increase time demand
   C. Sets and costumes followed by photo session
   D. Dress rehearsal with audience
   E. Opening night and run
   F. Wrap up

About the Contributor: *Will K. Andress is minister of music and arts at First United Methodist Church in Shreveport, Louisiana, where his music groups have performed many major works ranging from Bach's* St. Matthew Passion *and Mendelssohn's* Elijah *to Weber & Rice's* Jesus Christ, Superstar *and Schwartz's* Godspell. *He has been tenor soloist for the National Protestant Hour, a State Department Tour of the Far East, Radio City Music Hall,* *and has performed seven operatic roles. Will also sings in appearances with symphony orchestras, and completed a European recital tour in 1976. He has written and had published sixteen articles in* Opus II, *and forty-eight articles in* The Church Musician.

In his current church position he manages a program of over thirty music groups, a full orchestra, madrigal singers, a music theater, an apprentice program for church music majors, performances of several major works during the year, an annual arts festival, annual workshops featuring nationally known clinicians such as Jean Berger, Alice Parker, Jane Marshall and Erik Routley, and an involved program of children's, youth and adult choirs with groups touring worldwide.

As director of the Centenary College Choir, he conducts over sixty concerts annually, representing the Methodist College in Louisiana. This choir has also performed throughout Southeast Asia, the Soviet Union, and Europe in addition to most of the United States. This group has begun commissioning great American choral composers to write for their choir, including composers such as Samuel Adler, Jean Berger, Alice Parker, Emma Lou Diemer, Hank Beebe, and Richard Purvis. Will also teaches studio voice at Centenary College.

Besides earning a B.M. degree from Centenary College, an M.C.M. degree from Southern Baptist Seminary, an M.M. degree from East Carolina University, Will has received a D.M. degree from Florida State University. He has served as minister of music in five protestant churches ranging from one to six thousand members in Arkansas, North Carolina, Virginia, Florida, and Louisiana.

Dudley Blakeney

11.

Taped Accompaniment—Friend or Foe?

From the editor: *More and more publishers are making taped accompaniments available—fabulous instrumental recordings done in expensive studios with that special contemporary sound—just for choirs to sing with. Yet this very fact has brought about the need for a new kind of technical knowledge that isn't easy to find in a typical music curriculum in today's colleges and seminaries. Sound equipment, acoustics, conducting to a fixed tempo, all these new experiences must be dealt with in the best way possible.*

Dudley Blakeney has carefully considered the advantages and disadvantages of this kind of accompaniment and has put together some valuable thoughts about this relatively new area of church music. He has also included some practical information about rehearsal techniques, preparing yourself, getting the best sound and blend, and some performance helps.

The use of taped accompaniments is a growing trend in churches throughout America in recent years. More and more publishers are making fine tapes available. We ministers of music must decide one way or the other about whether taped accompaniment tracks are appropriate or practical for our specific congregations and choirs. There are plenty of opinions both in favor of and against this type of accompaniment.

Why Use Tracks?

The main arguments against using tapes concern technical performance risks. What if the tape breaks? What if the choir loses the tempo and speeds up or slows down? What kind of equipment is best and can my church afford it? How can the instrumentalists in my church have an opportunity to use their talent for God?

I was somewhat nervous when I first decided to try a choral performance with taped accompaniment because I had been trained to rely on that ever-following, all-fault-covering keyboard person to make smooth the rough places and find the lost beats. And with an accompanist I felt free to direct with my own ideas of tempo, rubato and interpretation.

Yet there were times when I sensed the limitations of not having more variety of instrumental colors than an organ or piano can provide. Some of my instrumentalists enjoyed the chance to sing in the choir. I had often felt the urge to introduce a variety of musical styles to the congregation which I knew were outside the range of my accompanists' interests or abilities.

My decision to begin using taped accompaniments, then, was made with the goal of adding variety of sounds and styles to our worship services while keeping a balance between this and the more traditional concept of keyboard accompaniment. After I began using "tracks," I found that they were a great tool for teaching rhythmic accuracy and good ensemble to the choir. The tapes actually save me money because I don't have to hire players from outside the church every time I want to use an orchestral accompaniment.

Another positive aspect of using tapes is that the freshness of this technique catches the ear of some people in the congregation in a way that the more traditional music in worship has not done. Some of them have said they usually "tuned out" before they had heard the message of the gospel. And, in some cases, it seemed to be just the right spice needed to perk up the old routine that had become a bit stale to others.

One of my choir members, who is also a very creative and talented person, said "I really like the variety that tracks give to the worship music. I really feel involved in the music and my mind doesn't wander to thoughts like next week's schedule or what the Cowboys' chances of winning are for this afternoon!"

Another member marveled at the capability of having an orchestra at the push of a button. He wondered, "Why would we ever need to bring in outside people again?"

I try to be flexible and sensitive to the feelings of my instrumentalists by giving them chances to use and develop their talents. And I feel that frequent use of taped accompaniments can get boring, can come across as rather plastic and can be irritating to some listeners. I try to keep a good balance so that each member of the congregation, choir and music staff is ministered to and no one is "left out" by the worship music.

When to Use Tracks

One of the best times to use tracks is when there is not much rehearsal time. But I choose an accompaniment tape for this situation carefully because some take a good deal of time to prepare well enough for the director and the choir to feel really confident. Other tracks, however, are quite simple and straightforward and can be used with little rehearsal time for the choir.

Another good occasion to use tracks is when there is not room for a large orchestra or there is no accompanist available. This has happened when I have sung for home weddings or parties. Just a small sound system or even a good tape deck makes a very satisfactory arrangement.

Other excellent times to use tracks when "live" accompaniment may be a logistical problem are for choir tours (particularly outdoors or in a small room), picnics, youth rallies, or possibly for a special touch on seasonal music.

Getting Familiar with the Track

I feel the essential element in using accompaniment tapes well is for me to be as familiar with the tape as possible *before* I first introduce it to the choir. I try never to introduce a tape to the choir until I feel that I am in control of the situation, which means knowing of any tempo changes, being able to handle any fermati that might occur and being aware of any dynamic changes or harmonic textures or problems that may require special attention. I *listen* to the track, with and without voices, and *follow* the vocal score until I achieve an "at home" feeling with the tempos so that there isn't a three-way struggle between me, the track, and the choir when we are in rehearsal. The number of times I listen and "shadow conduct" depends on the difficulty of the track.

A good way to handle a fermata is to listen through it several times, continuing to count in the last felt tempo. I mark my score with the number of beats contained. This may result in a 7/4 measure in the midst of a section of 4/4, but I am not guessing at where to give the cut-off.

Also, I mark places in the score that I might need as "landmarks" in case of trouble staying with the tempo, so I can get back on course. Typical landmarks are places where the instrumental sound changes (say, the brass comes in or a drum roll occurs between verses), or where the music begins again like the beginning. There may be a section where tempo is hard to feel for several beats, but if I know, and have marked in my score, that a strong drum beat falls on beat three, and I don't hear it until the upbeat of three, then I know I'm a half a beat ahead of the track and have a better chance of recovering, while the listeners are probably unaware of any problem. I try to remember to warn the choir of possible problem areas so that they can watch and follow me with extra care at those places.

Rehearsing the Choir

Once I feel prepared, the actual rehearsals with the choir are the next important step in preparing for a performance with a track. I play the track and let them listen through once to get a feel of things and then rehearse with a keyboard to nail the vocal lines down securely.

Whether or not I let the choir listen with the voices or without depends on how I feel about the style conveyed on the tape. Sometimes a choir can get into a style much more easily if they hear it sung by a good professional group. On the other hand, there may be some things that were done in the recording studio that I may not want the singers to imitate. Once they hear it one way, it may be difficult to change their interpretation of it.

If the track contains a lot of rubato, I often rehearse the choir *a capella,* using even more freedom to keep them following my direction closely when they sing with the tape.

For me, the best way to control the tape deck in rehearsal is by placing it within my reach, rather than having it controlled by someone else at a distance. This saves a lot of valuable time because I don't have another person to communicate with when I need to stop and start. I can also control the volume more satisfactorily. I make sure, however, to have at least one "dry run" in the actual room where we will perform with the sound technician at the controls. This is to get all of the balance problems between the sound track and the choir taken care of, and any adjustments needed for that particular room made.

During the "dry run," I want to be sure there is a good balance between the choir and the track from out in the congregation. A major aggravation I have run into concerning the use of tracks is when the words of the choir cannot be understood. I like to make sure that the levels are set so that the choir can hear well enough to sing securely and those listening can make out every word.

Sound Technicians

When working with a sound technician, it is very important that he or she have a good pair of ears as well as the ability to run the equipment. I give as clear an understanding of the balance that I want as I can during a "dry run." I comment on the sound while the technician makes the adjustments needed to bring the balance to the point that I feel is right. This can be done by standing beside him or her if your set-up permits. Another method is a set of hand signals agreed on ahead of time, or, as is the case in our church, an intercom may be used to make communication between the platform and the sound controls easier.

If at all possible, I place the technician so that he or she can hear what the congregation is hearing. A sheet of glass (as in a sound booth) between the technician and the source of sound is not helpful for live performance. Being in a closed sound booth is good only when the technician is monitoring sound for television or radio broadcast. The person who controls the taped accompaniment in live performance should be able to hear what the listeners present are hearing.

Equipment: Selection and Placement

After I feel comfortable with the tape and the choir has rehearsed with it, the effectiveness of the performance will depend on the quality of the equipment and how it is placed in the sanctuary or any other place where the choir is to sing. Microphones, tape decks, mixers and speakers all work together with the choir to produce a good blend and solid accompaniment for singers.

There are many fine mikes that work well for choirs. I recommend the Shure SM-58 (also a very good hand-held mike), the Electro Voice RE-10, or the AKG C451E. A new condenser mike that works very well for choir situations and is also much more durable than previous condensers is the Shure SM-81. These should be selected according to your needs and your particular situation. Some are more rugged than others (for travel on tours), and expense also varies a good deal. If the mike will be hand-held frequently, check for hand-noise sensitivity and the effects of the proximity of the singer on the tone quality. A salesperson in an audio equipment store in your area may advise you about these matters.

It is wise to check with other churches who have good quality systems to find what works for them, and then compare your situation to theirs. Whenever I have guest artists or groups in my church with equipment that seems to work particularly well in our building, I ask the sound technician about his or her set-up.

There are also seminars for church sound technicians given by groups like *Sound Investment Enterprises, Inc.*, run by Howard Parker, and having offices in Thousand Oaks, California, and Austin, Texas. These seminars are held all over the country and can be very helpful.

One problem that can really destroy a performance is feedback. This is a dissonant and sometimes ear-splitting tone that happens when sound from the speakers re-enters the microphone and goes back through the sound system and comes back out of the speakers. The noise created by this re-amplification is very unpleasant.

One thing that will help is to avoid omnidirectional microphones. Many people mistakenly believe that these make good choir mikes due to their pick-up pattern from all sides; however, this type of mike picks up as much unwanted noise around the room as it does the sound from the choir, and that may include the signal from the speakers. This type of mike will feed back quickly when the volume level is raised. Their primary use is for interview situations when a conversation between people opposite each other is being miked. (Lapel, or lavalier mikes are also of this type. They are *needed* at times, but care should be taken in their use with choirs.)

The acoustics of the room in which you are singing will have a great bearing on the feedback problem also. I try to stay with a good unidirectional (cardiod) mike which picks up from one basic direction. My control of the situation even in regard to miking some voices more than others, is much improved. Singers can be positioned in relation to the greater sensitivity areas of the microphone, according to their vocal strength.

There are advantages and drawbacks to consider when choosing between cassette and reel tape players. Some people prefer to use cassette decks because of the convenience of the size and weight of the tapes. This is especially helpful when there are only one or two numbers on the tape.

With professional quality machines, there is little difference between the two types, but I have found the reel to be somewhat more dependable and durable. I have used cassettes successfully, but I never feel quite as at ease about the situation because of the high casualty rate of those light-weight tapes. They tend to break more easily than tape on reels. I suggest that you take a good look at your own needs and budget and come to a decision that will best meet these.

Speaker placement will affect the ability of the singers to hear well enough to stay with the track, and also can cause feedback problems. The ideal situation is to have the P.A. speakers in front of the choir and the microphones and to have monitor speakers facing toward the choir and opposite the pick-up direction of the mikes. If the volume of the monitors can be controlled independently of the other speakers, that is even better.

If monitor speakers are not available, then the best place for the speakers is behind and slightly above the choir. In this position, the sound can reach the congregation and will travel by the singers first, thus allowing them to hear well enough to sing with confidence. Placing the speakers behind the choir can cause feedback, but by raising them high enough this problem can be greatly reduced or even done away with altogether, depending on the room's acoustics and the type of equipment being used.

If you don't like the way the speakers look, you may want to consider some sort of grill cloth to make them less distracting. Try to keep in mind though that to achieve the most "natural" or good quality sound the speaker signal must not be blocked by bodies, furniture, and so on. The "reflected" sound that results is usually not very complimentary.

Another matter I should mention is the use of a mixer. This is used to blend the sound from several mikes with the sound from the track. Normally there is one volume control for each input, which is a definite advantage over a single control for the entire sound. Not only can the balance between the track and the singers be more ideal, but blending problems within the group can be minimized as well. By experimenting (during the "dry run") I learn where the most "live" areas are, so I can rearrange the singers. This helps to tone down a "Tinny Tenor" or "Sliding Soprano" or possibly bring out the "Bashful Bass" with the nice tone by a little boost of one of the volume controls on the mixer.

But I try to be very cautious in placing singers, because this principle can work in reverse with disastrous results!

Singing with tracks can be a lot of fun both for the director and the members of the choir. The congregation enjoys it, too. I try to keep these points in mind: make sure the choir is well prepared and that the equipment is placed well and is the best the church can afford; see that the sound technician has a good knowledge of musical blend as well as technical ability with the equipment; and finally, don't overbalance your musical selections with too many taped accompaniment tracks.

***About the Contributor:** Dudley Blakeney holds a B.M. degree from Baylor University and has served as minister of music in three churches, including Bethel Baptist Church of Houston, Texas, First Baptist Church of Mt. Calm, Texas, and currently Calvary Baptist Church of Waco, Texas.*

His second vocation is studio singing. This has given him a good background in recording studio procedures which has helped him get good, tasteful results with accompaniment tapes and choirs.

Dudley's other interests are song writing and arranging music for himself and church groups, performing for various groups or functions, playing the guitar, playing tennis and taking walks with his wife, Emily, and their daughter, Corrie.

Neal Knighton

12.

Making a Musical Happen with Drama

***From the editor:** With the growing interest in major productions, particularly the presentation and staging of musicals, a little inside knowledge about drama is a help. Sometimes a musical will seem perfect for staging, yet knowing how to dramatize the story in a simple, yet meaningful way so that our volunteer actors and actresses can perform it well is often a problem.*

In my music training, I found little help with how to create drama, act it out, teach others to act, or direct. If you're in the same position, I think this chapter will help you to know where to start.

A major musical presentation is one of the most pleasant, yet powerful ways to penetrate the fog of resistance in many people's minds when they come to worship. It seems to me that worship is an area in which it is easy to let one's mind wander away from the subjects being presented in the service. So it follows that we as worship leaders can take advantage of various forms of communication to help attract attention and hold it. Adding drama to musicals, in which we can act out what the lyrics are revealing about God, can serve as a lighthouse beacon in the fog, by helping us to really "see" the ideas and concepts which we must otherwise rely on imagination to create.

Everything from a simple movement, like having the choir turn to watch a soloist during the solo, to elaborate musicals with staging, costumes and all the trimmings can be called "drama." I have been told that very little drama training comes with a basic music education, and since I have been a high school drama teacher who loves to do musicals, I would like to give you some of the basic drama ideas which I find helpful when planning a dramatic presentation. These will include such topics as dramatic movement ideas, structure and organization (like production crews—who does what) and some guidelines about costuming, makeup, set design, lighting and so on. Also included is a bibliography of sources which have helped me through the years, in case you want to get into more detail on your own. Even with a master's degree in this area and lots of reading, I have found that the best teacher has been experience.

Creative Drama—Choose It with Care

Some musicals are published with staging and drama ideas already created—some well presented and some only average. Other musicals are published with only the music, no drama at all, and yet the lyrics and story line lend themselves very nicely to dramatic interpretation. One rule of thumb that I've found helpful in all my drama planning is to try to keep the drama as simple as possible to convey the message powerfully. Simplicity seems to communicate much more strongly than complex and intricate scenes, gestures and so on.

One of the primary reasons for drama is to help the audience get to know the characters, so I choose dramatic movement for each character to help the personality of that character "come alive." For example, the cowardly and awkward Gideon might walk with an exaggerated bouncy-kneed swagger, and have his hands in his pockets most of the time, while keeping his gaze directed at the floor, the sky, his shoes, anywhere but at the person to whom he is talking. Then, after his realization that God will provide the necessary resources for his success, the change in his walk, his eye contact and strong hand gestures will help portray this character change.

Another thing I try to keep in mind is that any movement chosen to give meaning to a character must be motivated. By that I mean there must be a reason from within the story for it to happen. Gideon shouldn't just pace around to demonstrate the swagger unless there is a *reason* for him to be walking somewhere due to something in the story. Give some thought to the places in the story where the character is called upon to move naturally—then choose the appropriate actions for those movements. Some movement is usually necessary when there is an entrance by another character, a sound cue such as thunder, a ringing doorbell, a line spoken by someone else.

I have found that each character also has a certain tempo and emotional structure. Dramatic action is most effective when it is performed in the appropriate tempo for that character. For example, a big powerful fisherman like Peter may be deliberate and slow, while a wily tax collector like Matthew might be quick and nervous. Drawing all the characters together, each depending on the others for sympathetic interaction in their own individual actions and tempos will greatly enhance the dramatic effectiveness you can have.

Another thing I have to emphasize with my students is their need to exaggerate movements. What seems like a giant sweep of the arm to an inexperienced actor will often look like a swat at a mosquito from the audience. Heightening and exaggerating movement is helpful in getting the drama across well. Later, when a movement becomes more natural, toning it down is easier.

The role of a member of the crowd or someone in the background lending an ear to the action between the major characters is perhaps the most difficult role to play. An angry mob scene, for example, might include people shaking their fists up in the air, stalking around with angry frowns and so on. Yet to have the entire group simultaneously shaking their fists on beat three of the fourth measure would distract and amuse the audience and would not be as effective as spacing such actions more randomly. I usually think of five or six actions that would be appropriate and suggest them all to the group. Then they practice using them enough so that no one duplicates the actions of any of his or her neighbors. Then I encourage them once again to *exaggerate* those actions and do them slowly enough to be seen from the audience.

One area of terminology with which it helps to be familiar is that of stage directions. If you and the choir are all familiar with these terms, then it is much easier for you to direct an actor. All stage direction should be dictated from the perspective of the actor when facing his or her audience. When we all understand these notations, an actor can know where I want him or her located or to move. The following diagram labels the areas of the stage:

Diagram of Stage Positions

Backstage

up right	up right center	up center	up left center	up left
right	right center	center stage	left center	left
down right	down right center	down center	down left center	down left

Audience

Some other factors I take into consideration when planning are the "strength" areas of the stage. Major characters need strong entrances, and key lines should be delivered from strong areas of the stage. The following diagram shows the areas I believe to be the strength areas, number one being the strongest and then descending in order of importance.

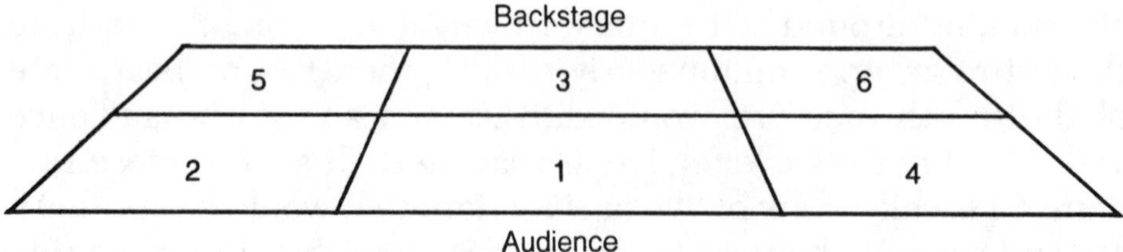

This diagram shows my preferences, but of course the type of stage used and the auditorium arrangement will contribute to your own choices for staging. When planning the entrances and exits, keep in mind that down stage entrances or exits are usually considered very weak because an actor must advance several steps to capture the attention of the audience. Up stage entrances are much stronger in their effect, the strongest of all being an entrance or exit U.C. (up center).

The third diagram indicates body positions on the stage. I try to be specific when telling an actor that he or she is turned too far in one direction or another, and since all the actors are familiar with these terms, I find that things are much easier to explain.

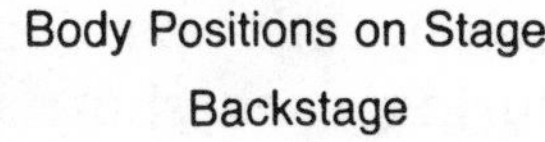

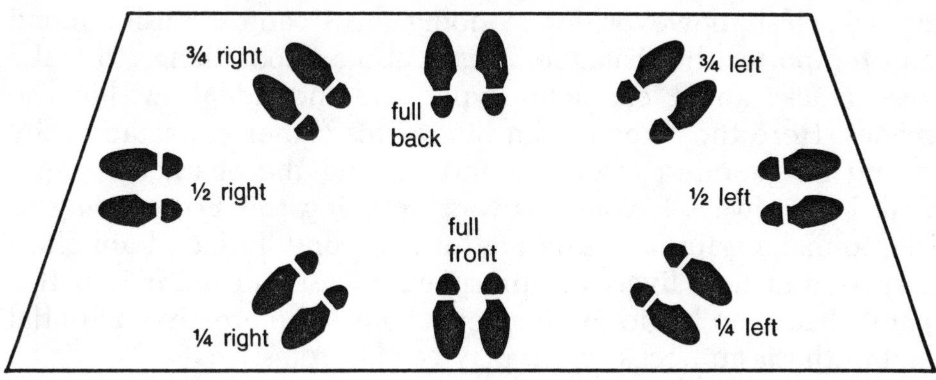

Directing Effectively

If you have decided to be the director of the drama as well as the music, then your role will include planning the dramatic movement, teaching it to the actors, choosing the actors, being in charge of all other members of the production crew and moving the entire cast, choir and crew toward an emotional high point similar to the high point in the actual story line. In my opinion, theatrical or directing experience is not nearly as important for you as the director as are your sensitivity and managerial skills. It is feasible, however, to delegate the role of director and have that person be responsible to you for approval on all the drama choices. He or she should conduct the drama rehearsals and then be available in full rehearsals to cover drama questions and be in charge of the rest of the crew. If you choose to do this, your director might read through this chapter after you finish it to get some ideas of the structural basis for the two of you working together.

Preparing the Actors

Choosing the most appropriate person to play each role is a major part of the dramatization of a musical. It is often my most difficult task. First, I make the entire script available for review by every interested person. A reading and general discussion is to me an easy way to accomplish this, with different people reading the various parts. This gives me a chance to see the possible cast members in the early stages of understanding the story.

During this reading I really enjoy participating myself by taking one part or another during each short reading. My motive is not all selfish, however, for by doing this I can establish a mood and tempo for the dialogue. This is also a good chance to make wise cracks about character types and individuals within the scenes. Here the director can hint at his or her expectations by giving exaggerated examples and making the characters seem real. I am always looking for ways to bring this first reading to life, to make it fun and exciting for everyone. In fact, I am often surprised at how lively my prospective cast can be! It is at this point that I can begin to discover who has the creative potential and enthusiasm necessary to play certain roles.

Generally, fumbling lines or missing pronunciation and cues is not important in this reading. Only the spirit and movement of the story should be understood.

At the second meeting the prospective cast should come prepared to try out, having known in advance, for instance, that all persons interested in the parts of Gideon and Joash should be fully aware of their lines in Scenes III and IV. After a number of similar tryouts for the other major characters, I make my choices.

There are a few basic guidelines I try to use when finally choosing the cast. General physical fitness, adaptability of the actor to his or her role, voice quality, pitch, age and apparent emotional grasp of the part are all important to me. But I feel strongly that the actor's attitude toward the group and his or her own ability to cooperate is an important key to my choosing him or her for the part. I have learned that the rigors of production can place high demands on every cast and crew member and can often demand only a little less than military discipline and dependability. I almost always require each prospective cast member to sign a pledge of support for the schedule of rehearsals which will be required.

An interesting paradox, however, is that often the biggest cut-ups or discipline problems, perhaps because of their personalities and experience, will often be the best actors of all. Giving them a part with some real "meat" to it can make them invaluable to the production rather than a hindrance. On the other extreme, quite shy individuals sometimes become truly outstanding and open when given a character to "hide" behind.

Once my decisions have been made, then comes the challenge of preparing these actors and actresses for performance time. One of the biggest drawbacks that can beset a young and inexperienced actor (or an older one, for that matter!) is stage fright. Two things can help overcome this: attitude and confidence.

One way I try to help actors and actresses with their attitude is by telling them that in my eight years of experience in teaching and directing, I have found that almost everyone is afraid of being laughed at or considered silly while performing, especially in front of peers or friends. One way I've found helpful to approach this feeling in myself is to think of the nature of acting, which is: when I am playing the part of a character, this means *I* am not trying to "be myself" in front of people. I really am pretending to be someone else, and so I have a mask to hide behind.

As a character, I can say or do my part in almost any way I choose, but I am not Neal Knighton anymore, and while I am "inside the character's skin," I want the audience to really see Gideon, or Paul, or whoever I am playing, and to *hide* Neal Knighton. It is not me *acting like* I'm Gideon, it is Gideon who must come out of me to appear before the audience. This helps me to be able to laugh or cry with the character I portray knowing that the bigger, sometimes more exaggeratedly I play the part, the further removed I become from my own personality.

Now for confidence—that sure feeling that comes with knowing what you are doing. There are several stages in getting comfortable with a role. The first is getting to know the character. I believe that each actor should look at his or her character as if they were good friends about whom they knew everything. I often give my actors the following questions to ask about their character to help in this getting acquainted process:

1. Can I list adjectives used to describe my character (20 or more)?

2. What are my character's physical characteristics (such as race, nationality, age, strength, carriage, movements, speech and dress)?

3. What are my character's mental characteristics (such as native intelligence, thinking habits, education, originality and awareness)?

4. What are my character's emotional characteristics (such as basic attitudes: likes and dislikes toward life)?

5. Does he or she show sensitivity toward others (such as capacities for deep feeling, stability, and self control)? How?

6. What are his or her social characteristics (such as social class, economic status, religion, profession, and daily routines)?

After this familiarization time, I begin to teach the dramatic actions I have in mind. For each scene, I draw up a diagram of the stage with the set pieces, doors, windows, and so on, marked. I indicate with arrows the direction the character should move at given moments. Each one can see where he or she is to go individually. And the actors working together in a scene can see how they interact with each other. The next diagram shows how I do this. Similar scenes may not need such diagrams, but studying such a "picture" really helps cut down on confusion, "forgetfulness" and so on.

The following is a rough diagram that I might use to begin my rehearsals.

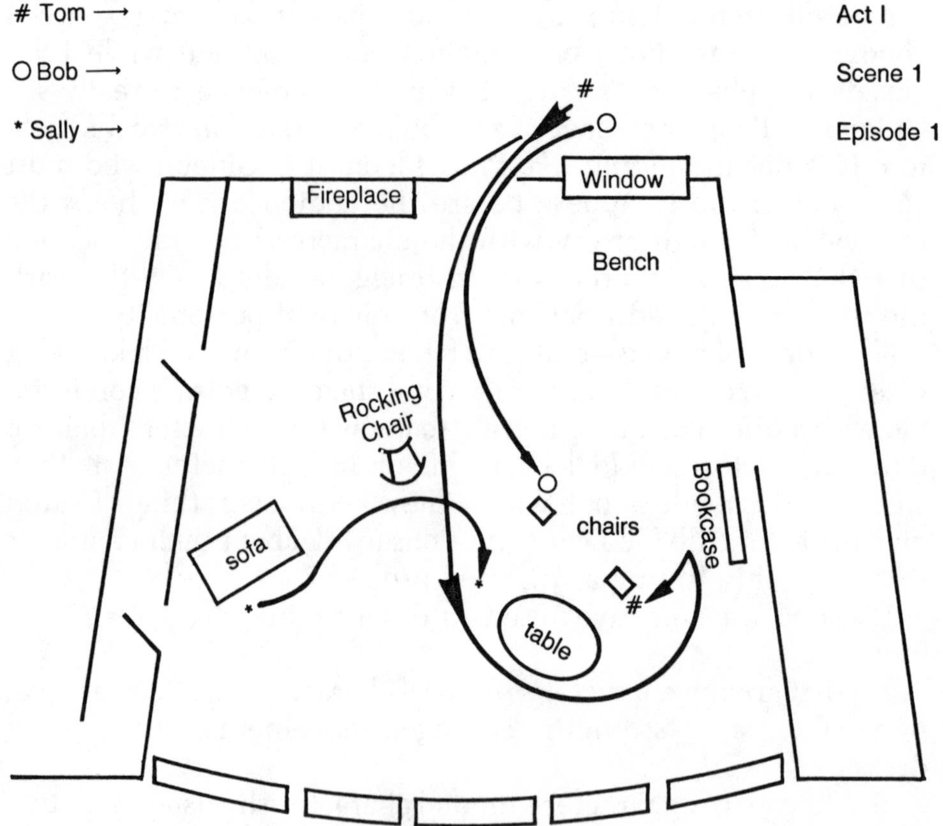

Other helpful diagrams are those of the stage for each scene change. I include all set pieces and properties, and make notes about who moves what pieces and where they are to be stored when not in use. I also make lighting plots to show the lighting effects I want. Copies of these diagrams go to the appropriate people in charge of properties, sets, lights, and so on, while I keep the master copies in my director's script.

All of these directions come from the master diagrams, including everybody's movement or assignments, which I have prepared in advance and placed between the pages of my script.

Of course, all preliminary planning, especially the movement of the actors, is subject to change, but I can't tell you how much easier rehearsals can be when the preparation has already been completed.

This technique has saved enormous amounts of time during rehearsal and also has helped with the respect of the cast and crew. It allows the crew to begin its work early and know why they are doing the things they are doing. I give individual members of the cast blank diagrams of the stage for each scene in which they are a part so that they can pencil in with arrows the lines of their own movement.

After the actors have become familiar with their characters and have a basic idea of the movements I have planned, the last phase of gaining confidence is rehearsals. It is helpful to consult the calendars for information about school, civic and church events, then plan the entire schedule of rehearsals right at the beginning. Copies of the schedule are passed out with the scripts even before the cast is chosen. The number of rehearsals varies according to the size of the musical. I usually plan a minimum of six rehearsals for a shorter production and fifteen for a longer one (three acts). I try not to place them too far apart, usually with two or three two-hour rehearsals per week. I also schedule work time for the stage crew separately from the regular rehearsals. The valuable time of your work crews can be managed much better this way.

The rehearsals seem to be the thing most remembered and most often discussed, so I try to make them fun by establishing a light hearted, easy-going style. I might as well put off being a crazy, hair-pulling perfectionist tyrant as long as I can. Ha! Ha!

In addition to the schedule for rehearsals, I put other things in writing, too. From the first rehearsal to the last, I want to have some idea where everyone is to be and what they should be doing at all times, whether it be for the most important member of the cast or the least active member of the crew.

The Production Crew

One of the most important teams of people is the production crew. Without these nine people there is no way that the schedules and diagrams can be carried out. I choose these people carefully and explain to each one clearly what his or her responsibility will be. Then I rely on that person to carry out the job with minimal supervision.

Here is a list of the nine positions which make up the production crews:

1. Assistant Director: To help the director in any way possible.
2. Business Manager: To handle all the business arrangements. This person schedules the stage for rehearsals and performances, chooses ushers, is responsible for programs, keeps accurate account of all receipts and expenditures, sees that the house is adequately ventilated and free from excess noise.
3. Publicity Manager: To get the audience. He or she should consider the age and educational level of the musical, the emotional theme and therefore the mood of the advertising campaign.*
4. Stage Manager: To handle the set, stage, curtains, major set pieces (i.e. furniture), and properties, as well as cleanliness and general appearance of the house. Also he or she supervises all movement during scene changes and should be someone who can make quick decisions and give orders politely but firmly and authoritatively. The cast and crew (sometimes even the director!) should see his or her word as *law.*
5. Lighting Manager: To handle lighting both on stage and in the audience.
6. Properties Manager: To list, secure, organize, dispense and return all of the necessary properties, including making them available during rehearsal.
7. Prompter: To be present at every rehearsal and constantly hold the director's script with all the production notes. The prompter should see that the director is free to move and work with the cast and crew as well as take notes that the director might need to use later.
8. Costume Manager: To secure costumes for each character in the production. Costumes must be ready at least one week before production and then they should be used in rehearsal.
9. Make-Up Manager: To be reponsible for all make-up used in the production. He or she must work closely with the costume manager and lighting manager.

Each manager has his or her own crew, as needed, according to the size of the production. I schedule lighting and sound re-

---

* See Chapter 15 for more details about advertising campaigns.

hearsals after the lines are well learned and blocking and set pieces are well established. Though the cast members may be the "stars," it is the crew that makes them "shine." Try to be careful not to waste the time of the crew.

Set Design

Designing sets especially for a sanctuary staging is sometimes a tricky job. Two criteria I hold as primary are that the sets must be light weight and available for quick movement. These are basic. I have used cardboard, hung drapes from temporary battens, or hung a canvas backdrop, or even rented full scenery, being careful not to interfere with other scheduled events like funerals and weddings.

The third criteria is the most important to me. That is that the sets must be imaginative. Drama, by its very nature, is meant to be "seen" in the mind of the audience and through their imaginations actually appear before them. Try to stimulate the imagination of the viewers and involve them by making them think. I've been known to use people lined up to represent a wall or a train, doors, curtains and many other things as well. I've turned furniture upside down to represent trees and bushes. I've used empty boxes and stacked them to become cars and trucks. Ladders can make great trees as well as giants, boats, or space ships. Audiences almost always respond to a new and different use of some ordinary piece of furniture or paraphernalia.

Lighting

I have mentioned stage lighting several times already, but I would like to suggest a few more specific ideas. Changes in lighting serve several purposes. One purpose is to show the time of day; therefore, the lighting must be consistent with the time intended for the plot. For example, bright lights for late morning or early afternoon, more subdued lighting for evening and early morning and darker lighting for night time—even on indoor scenes.

Another purpose is to emphasize a character or scene. Also, lighting changes the moods present on stage and offers a means of shifting emotions or changing the level of the emotional involvement of the audience. Lighting should as nearly as possible appear to be originating from a natural source, and like natural light it should vary with intensity in various areas of the stage. Subtle color shading is particularly important for this. And yet, drastic light changes may be used, such as a sudden blackout to represent a closing curtain.

The following color chart is helpful when choosing colors for the lighting plots. Keep in mind that draperies, costumes, carpets and walls might change the true color of a light and its normal reflection. When it comes to our final decisions, I rely on my light manager's sense of color and my own view when seeing all our set pieces, costumes and background colors together.

Color	*Emotion*	*Effect*
red	excitement	heat
amber	cheerful	warmth
small concentration of yellow	optimism	sunny and bright
general yellow lighting	sickness	jaundice, sickly character
small concentration of green	hope	growth and nature
general green lighting	weird	cold, unearthly effect
reflected blue	joy	clear skies
general blue lighting	cheerless	cold
purple	suffering	sickness
gray	sadness	cold

In working with colors, remember that the shadow cast by a colored light has its own color, usually the complementary color of the original light according to the color wheel below. For example, the shadow of an object in blue light will have orange tints.

COLOR CHART

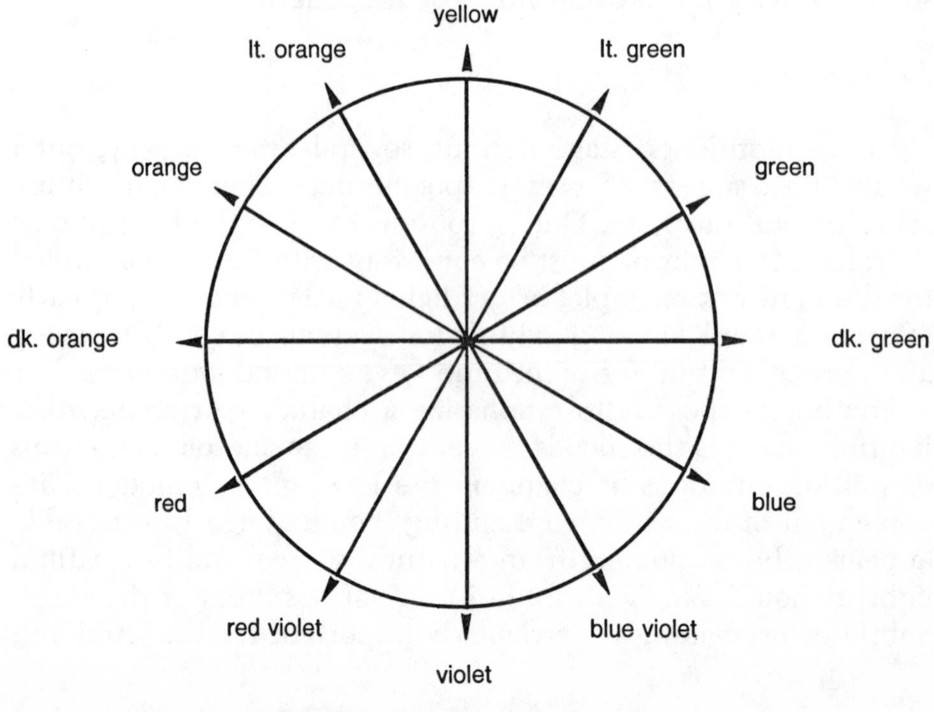

Complementary Colors Are Opposite

Plan lighting plots with two types of lighting in mind: general and specific. "General" lighting is most commonly done with a strip or trough of lights anywhere from four to eight feet in length. It has alternating colors of red, blue, amber and sometimes green. They are called footlights (when attached to the floor on the apron of the stage), border lights (when attached horizontally from a batten behind your border curtains), and strip lights (when stood or suspended in the wings of the stage.)

It is easy to build a set of strip lights by placing sockets in a trough four to five inches apart and running one common wire to each socket with a separate wire running to each color of light in sequence (one wire connecting all the blue lights, another for all the reds, and so on). Attach each wire to a rheostat or dimmer switch for control by the light manager. The best plan is to have a separate compartment for each bulb and cover these with colored glass or tinted plastic gel.

"Specific" lighting is done with various kinds of spotlights including large "follow spotlights" which have their own stand and will freely rotate in any direction, "baby spotlights" which are usually hung on the stage itself, and "floodlights" which are suspended or aimed to give an intense diffused light. The "follow spots" are used offstage to cast a strong beam of light for some distance. "Baby spots" are designed for concentrated lighting at a short distance and can be used to cast light from various angles to create contrasting shadows. Some accessories for baby spots include colored gel frames or screens and a "stove pipe" which is a cylindrical item that helps to concentrate the beam of light. Floodlights are often used to represent sunshine or a bright source of light.

Ask your lighting manager to make a list of the lights you have available already, then plan additional lights you will need. He or she can then contact rental agencies and also places where lights can be purchased to get costs for the added lights. After consulting with your business manager or the budget committee of the church, you can then know what kind of lighting will be available and have a better idea of how to plan.

For the final rehearsals and performances, I feel it is necessary to put the switchboard in a place where the light manager will be able to see the action on stage at all times, and I recommend that the same switchboard be used to control the house lights if possible. Dimmer units allow great flexibility, but if switches are to be used, try to avoid those that make a noise or click.

To compute the electrical capacity of your stage and/or auditorium, first locate all the electrical outlets. (If, after reading the rest of this paragraph you decide it is too complicated, you can probably find someone in your congregation who would really like to help you). These are usually labeled with their amperage and volt rating. Next, multiply the number of amps by the number of volts to find out the total number of watts that the circuit will carry. Also the circuit breakers or fuses located in the power distribution panel will indicate the number of amps which can be drawn on a particular circuit. Normally all circuits other than those intended for large appliances are rated at 110 volts and 25-40 amps.

A church auditorium is usually small enough to use 100-250-500 watt bulbs (the normal theater will use 1000-1500 watt bulbs). Don't be misled. You can coordinate a lighting system for your auditorium. Almost any church member with electrical experience, or a good "do-it-yourselfer" should be able to give you all the help you will need.

In working out the lighting plot, I usually begin my plans with the "specific" sources of light. I consider the audience's view from every area of the house and test out all the spotlights and floodlights using the actors and actresses as they move through their blocking instructions. In advance I aim each light in the general area I will be using it. Of course, changes are always needed and may be easily accomplished in a rehearsal specifically for this purpose. After the spots and floods have been aimed and set, "general" lighting is then gradually introduced to tie together each scene and the actors and actresses.

Properties

The properties (or "props," for short) you will need will be fairly obvious from the text of your story. The thing I have learned about using props in a drama is that mistakes can be minimized when the actors have had lots of rehearsal time to practice using them (after all, Murphy's Law was created in public performance). Getting the props together early in the rehearsals, even before sets, costuming, lights and so on are begun, will help. Secondhand stores and garage sales are excellent sources for many prop and costume needs.

Costuming

When it comes to costumes, I find that simple garments are usually the key to making a costume effective on stage. A costume should always be a symbol of the character wearing it. Whether producing a period play or a modern symbolic parable, keep in mind that the clothing of the characters will help put the time period across. Don't try to compete with museum collections, but try to create the flavor of the period of time with which you are working. If you want to produce a musical about Gideon, yet show that his kind of fear and feelings of low self-worth are also found in men and women of today, then use modern costumes. Otherwise, go back through Bible history books and see what is depicted as authentic in Gideon's time.

Concerning color, costumes and their color are determined from the setting and the text of the story. Dark backgrounds call for brighter costumes, and the reverse is true. I use lots of color in the costumes of major characters to bring them out, and use quieter colors on the minor ones. Other items of costuming which can help characterize a personality include jewelry, hats and small props. Audiences expect the bad guy to be in dark colors. Don't be afraid to use stereotype and universal appeal when they are appropriate.

I usually try to choose inexpensive fabrics, always avoid having to cut the inside seams, and try to sew everything with wide stitches so I can adapt most costumes for a later production.

After each play, have the costume manager get all the costumes cleaned and stored carefully so they'll be ready for their next use.

One inexpensive way to handle costumes in a modern play is for each member of the cast to wear clothing from his or her own wardrobe.

For those hard-to-depict characters, there are rental companies with costumes available. It might be the making of your musical if the main character or two had costumes that were really "right," thus giving the rest of the costumes a feeling of authenticity.

The costume manager should be asked to schedule all scenes and list what costumes will be required for each character. He or she should approve any items that come from a person's own wardrobe, help make suggestions, contact rental agencies if need be, and make sure everything is ready by at least one week prior to performance. And last, but never unimportant, is what I consider the costume manager's main responsibility: to be backstage prepared with safety pins, needles, thread and immodesty!

Make-Up

The use of stage make-up is an art, yet it is an art that can be learned. The best teacher is, of course, practical experience.

The reason for make-up is that bright lights and distances from the stage tend to wash out the natural color in the face and skin. We use make-up so that the players will appear natural to the audience. If at any time a character seems unreal or fake, chances are that you are using *too much* make-up. *BEWARE!!* It is better to have too little than too much!

There are two basic types of make-up. Straight make-up is used for normal everyday roles while character make-up is used to change the physical characteristics of the actor or actress.

The order of application for both types of make-up is exactly the same. The skin must first be clean and dry. An application of cold cream should always be used to keep the make-up from being absorbed into the skin. For an actor with very little make-up, or make-up that must remain on for only a short period of time, cosmetic medicated make-up may be applied. This is usually water soluble, and easy to remove even with colored rouge or pencil on top.

Next will be the use of a foundation make-up. Water soluble "pancake" is available in a variety of shades. Foundation grease paints are widely used. Be careful to spread the foundation make-up over all the exposed areas of an actor's body. The neck, ears, hands and hairline are especially important and often forgotten.

The age of a character will help determine the right color of your foundation make-up. Basically age brings lighter, more pale or yellow skin. The hue of an individual's natural complexion will sometimes alter the color of his or her make-up. So I recommend that you experiment to see what is best for each character.

The third step is the use of rouge or color sticks for the cheeks and lips. Men must always be careful not to use too much color on their lips. The tendency is to leave the lips too broad or full. (Gentlemen, a helpful hint is that a light coating of base make-up on the lips will make them much easier to clean after the show.)

The use of make-up should be determined for each character, according to the intensity of your lighting. You should always utilize the "character lines" (wrinkles) which each actor naturally has. Accentuate these lines with eye liner and light shades of eye shadow to bring brightness and size to the character's eyes. As age increases, the cheeks begin to drop and sag, below usually weak eyes. Weak eyes may be shown with a white or red line drawn next to the lashes.

Aging a character is an easy task. Simply remember that lips seem to become dark and thin and cheek bones (shown with rouge) take the shape of triangles. Wrinkles must always be very sharp lines which are blended into the foundation at their ends. Wrinkles around the eye should not come too close to the outer edges of the eyes. I like to allow a pencil width before drawing in the popular "crow's-feet."

After all the make-up is in place, a powder should be used to soften the face. This may, if necessary, be followed by touch-up coloring for the cheeks and lips. I always try to test all make-up early in the production schedule and view it critically under the lighting to be used on stage.

Resources

As I mentioned earlier, I am including a list of publications which have helped me plan staging, be a director and organize all the details involved in presenting a dramatic work. I have condensed some of my experiences and learning into a few pages and hope that it will help you in your thinking about adding dramatic action to musical productions.

Buch, Arthur T. *The Bible on Broadway.* New York: Archon Books, 1968.

Carroll, Sydney W. *Acting for the Stage: Art, Craft and Practice.* New York: Pitman Publishing Corp., 1938.

Eastman, Fred and Wilson Louis. *Drama in the Church.* New York: Samuel French, 1942.

Ehrensperger, Harold. *Religious Drama: Ends and Means.* New York: Abingdon Press, 1962.

Welker, David. *Theatrical Direction—The Basic Techniques.* Boston: Allyn and Bacon Inc., 1971.

Wright, Edward A. and Downs, Lenthier H. *A Primer for Playgoers.* Englewood Cliffs, N.J.: Prentice-Hall, 1969.

About the Contributor: *Neal Knighton holds a B.S. in Education as well as an M.A. in Oral Communication from Baylor University. He taught drama and speech at the high school level directing plays and tournament activities. He also taught at the junior high level. One of his special interests is adapting literature to dramatic form.*

Neal has also been a lecturer at the college level, teaching courses in "Business and Professional Speaking" and "Speech as a Communication Skill." He also served as co-director of the National High School Interpretation Workshop sponsored by Baylor University, Waco, Texas. At the present time Neal is minister to college and single adults at the First Baptist Church of Columbia, South Carolina.

Neal's other interests include church drama, creative worship services, sports, carpentry, teaching a high school age Sunday school class, civic drama and music.

Lee White

13.

"Show and Sing" with Slides

***From the editor:** One striking way to capture the attention of your audience is by illustrating what you are singing with slides. Not only do you "tell" them the good news, you "show" them.*

If someone in your choir or congregation is a good amateur photographer with a creative flair, why not harness that talent into a multimedia experience? It could be the perfect touch to an Easter anthem, or an entire musical, or an evening concert.

Lee White is an amateur photographer who has done some professional assignments. The story of how he started with one of his first shows would be excellent reading for the amateur photographer(s) you have available to you. This exciting method of expanding your ministry could make a big difference.

I had never been to a World's Fair. Then in 1968, shortly after my graduation from high school, I went to see Hemisfair in San Antonio. Being around all those rides, exotic booths, and the crowds of people from around the world, made those three days an unforgettable experience.

One building in particular holds a place in my memory. The Institute of Texan Cultures had an audio-visual exhibit featuring a new mechanical innovation—the dissolve control. Visitors sat on the floor looking up into a black recess in the ceiling. Into that recess had been built a dozen projection screens of varying size. When the show began, selected screens lit up, sometimes on opposite sides of the room, mixing slides and occasionally

16mm in glimpses of the variety of cultures in Texas. There was something unusual about the slides, though. Instead of the usual black gap on the screen between slides, there was a rhythmic blending from one slide to the next; as one faded out the next appeared. I left the exhibit, fascinated by what I had seen, and filed the experience away in my memory bank for future reference.

Several years later, while sitting in an evening service at a small Presbyterian church, I listened as the preacher paraphrased the story of the prodigal son in a modern setting. In my mind I was visualizing scenes. As I left the service, I asked myself why this couldn't be done on film, complete with contemporary music. Thus began a simple idea that blossomed into a series of multimedia programs over the next five years.

The worship experience in many churches underwent some dramatic changes in the 1970s. One of the greatest has been in the area of music. Fresh new music from people like Ralph Carmichael, John Fischer and Bill Gaither is taking its place beside the great hymns of the church. People involved in music and worship planning are searching for new ways to enhance the worship experience, and an area that is enjoying increased popularity is photography.

How do you put together an audio-visual program? Doesn't it require professional experience? Is it expensive? Where do you begin? It begins with an idea, a concept—a message.

Most of my programs began with the greatest "Idea Book" ever written—the Bible. From it I select a story, or I might choose an idea around which a story can be built, such as sacrifice, or love, or the Ten Commandments.

For my first experiment, I chose the parable of the prodigal son, because it is a classic example of forgiveness and the quality of love God has for his children. To relate this story to a modern generation, I updated the story, moving it to a ranch in Texas, with the son leaving his father's house for a "big" city. In this case it was Corpus Christi. The flow of the story must be thought through, possibly writing out an outline of the dramatic action. It might look something like this:

Develop characters: father—wise, respected, wealthy
older son—hard worker, quiet, solitary
young son—life of the party, center of action

Son leaves home, goes to city, spends money on cars, clothes, fancy apartments, parties. . . . Meanwhile life continues on farm, with father always watching for his son's return. Son finds that his new life does not satisfy, longs for his father's house, sets out to walk home. Father sees him, runs to meet him, throws party. Older son resents brother until father confronts him. Brothers are reunited, story ends with thought: Who do you, the viewer, relate to?

With this rough outline I moved to a critical ingredient of the program: the music which would be used to set the mood and tempo of the story. One of the big new Christian groups on the scene at the time was "Love Song," and their music seemed to fit the story perfectly, so I chose songs like "Two Hands" and "Love Song." There are contemporary secular artists who have music with a message, and I don't think we should hesitate to use some of it. Jim Croce is a case in point, or Bob Dylan. "Try a Little Kindness" amplified the message of the father to the unforgiving older brother.

The musicians for this program were a couple of singing guitarists. They arranged the music and tied it together. The three of us got together, and while listening to the music, visualized the action, making a list of any ideas we came up with. I remember spending one whole Saturday with Hershall and Mike Seals in their garage, playing the same songs over and over. I had never worked with them before, but had heard them do a couple of Girard's songs, and decided that they were the ones to do the music for this program.

The next step in developing a program was the photography. Really all that is required is a 35mm camera, a basic knowledge of photography, and a little creativity. I had met a professional photographer, Dale Smothers, while visiting a church and shared this idea with him. He invested a couple of days and several rolls of film in the project, as well as a wealth of technical skill. Dale got caught up in this idea of illustrating a story from the Bible with slides and music. (A couple of years later he put together a set of slides to accompany his church's youth choir when they performed Paul Johnson's *Here Comes the Son.*)

Picking subjects for slides can be difficult. Scenery is the easiest subject: landscapes, sunsets, and so on, but viewers relate best to other people. With that in mind I cast the story. For the "Prodigal" story, I chose two high school boys to play the brothers, and a man to play the father. There were also extras for the homecoming, but these three were my key subjects. After the three understood the whole idea, they began getting into their roles. The characters were talking during the shooting, even to the point of making up lines.

Shooting was awkward at first, until everyone got comfortable being around the camera. Since the story had to be told in slides, every shot had to communicate something to the viewer. To illustrate solitude we shot the boy walking down an old railroad track at sundown. To give the effect of movement we shot him hitchhiking down a crowded highway, the passing cars only a colored blur.

The most exciting shots occurred as the boy was returning home, and that moment of reunion is possibly one of my favorite series of pictures. The camera was behind the father, looking over his shoulder and focused on the face of the returning son as he walked up the road to the house. That series of five slides carries great emotional impact, but took a whole roll of film to shoot.

That brings up an important point: take plenty of pictures. It's hard to tell what they will look like until you get them back from the developer. By then it's too late to recreate a setting. It's better to have too many shots and throw away a few than have to make do with a shot that is less than perfect.

For the next few weeks I carried my camera everywhere, watching for things that might or might not work into the story. If I couldn't use them, I saved them for future use.

Finally I sat down to edit and arrange the slides, organizing first by subject in piles, then composing a visual story. Two major items are needed for this. It is best to have plenty of room to spread out slides. If it's done on a table, I use slips of paper to label the various piles. The second item is a slide sorter, which can be purchased at any photography store for under $10.00. Here I arrange them in order, following the original story outline. Once arranged, I number them in consecutive order. The "Prodigal" consisted of about 280 slides, but it took nearly 500 slides to get there.

At this point, the type of projection equipment becomes important. Since I use a Kodak 760 system, I placed the slides in two carousels, 140 in each, with all odd numbers in one and even numbers in the other. The carousels fit my two self-focusing projectors, which were coupled to a Kodak Dissolve Control unit. This unit can be set to automatically forward slides, alternating between projectors. My projectors are equipped with wide-angle lenses which makes it possible to keep them very close to the screen for optimum light and clarity.

Then with the musicians present, we all watched the slides and worked at synchronizing music and pictures. Slides can still be changed or rearranged until the desired effect is achieved. It is always helpful for the musicians or choir to see the screen.

Hershall, Mike and I spent another full day polishing the "Prodigal." I had written a simple narration to move the story along. This presented audio problems since I was unaccustomed to using a microphone. With some coaching from Mike, I learned how to hold it, and we managed to get the sound balanced.

Our first showing was to be at my church. Nobody really knew what to expect as the crowd began to gather in the fellowship hall of the church. It got off to an awkward start, but then began to flow more smoothly. The result that evening was an electrifying worship experience. The three of us had a difficult time completing the performance; we had become totally absorbed in the experience. A lump rose in my throat as the prodigal returned home, and I had to strain to speak the last lines of the story. As the lights came back on, I noticed moist eyes all about the room. The congregation had been as caught up in the story as we had.

From this rather simple beginning, ideas were generated for a whole series of parables, for musicals, for teaching programs. The concept can be expanded to elaborate programs using multiple screens. The possibilities are endless.

I have mentioned what I use in my programs. A simple system might consist of the following:

2 Kodak 760-H projectors
1 Kodak Dissolve Control
(Bell and Howell also makes an excellent dissolve unit which works with Kodak projectors.)

A projection screen is necessary, but can be either the tripod variety, a wall hung model, or one of the elaborate rear-projection screens. These are great for classroom use. I have seen several homemade models which consist of a white bedsheet stretched over a wood frame. This works great for rear projection, keeping equipment out of sight.

The use of electronic audio-visual media is doing for modern worship what stained glass did for the Gothic cathedrals of Europe. It is an artistic expression of faith and praise that speaks of the creativity of the living Lord. It enhances public worship and inspires the participant. With this basic knowledge of multimedia, all that remains is to go forth and be creative.

About the contributor: *Lee White is the Vice President of Toland Construction Co., Inc. in Taft, Texas, and holds a B.A. in Political Science from Sam Houston State University. He has produced several multimedia programs since 1972 and has worked on photographic projects for the Southwest Texas Conference of the United Methodist Church and Joint Effort Leisure Ministries in Corpus Christi, Texas. Lee is a member of First United Methodist Church in Taft.*

Cam Floria

14.

Going on the Road

***From the editor:** It's summer time again, and the kids are out of school. With no homework, tests, papers and other school pressures to get in their way, they are perhaps freer than at any other time of the year to become closely involved in a church program. One way that is both fun and educational is to involve them in a tour.*

Then again, maybe your adult choir is made up of adventuresome people who want to share the gospel through music and personal contact with others. Why not organize a three-day or week-long tour for them?

I have even heard of churches who combine the high school choir members with adult choir members to provide an interesting variety of musical presentation, plus built-in chaperones for the young people and a model for creativity and energy for the adults—a combination which makes each age group more than it might have been alone!

But all this can sound easier to do than it is without some guidelines to follow and experience from which to learn.

A long time ago I realized there were many reasons for taking tours. There's the basic fun of travel and being in new places; the excitement of being with a new audience and hearing their applause; the showing of love for God by actually doing something to carry out his plan of evangelization. "Go," he said, so "going" makes sense to me. But of all the reasons and after all the years, it all comes down to the effect on the choir person who goes, and the meaning it has for him or her. In other ministries they call it discipleship training. I don't have a better term, so just keep that one in mind.

One other thought that constantly comes to me is this: When I became a Christian, God did not whisk me away to heaven—he left me here to do something! My ministry is music, and to me that includes the conviction that every song, every lyric, every idea, every program and production, has as its *ultimate* direct goal to present the gospel again and/or inspire and build up others to do the same.

Do you want to take a tour? Why? It's an awful lot of work! If it's going to be a *really* good experience for the choir, the people they perform for and you, then it could be the hardest thing you have ever pulled off in your entire life.

But before you become discouraged, let me say that it is possible to have a successful experience, if you are first willing to pay the price. Of all the things you can do with music groups, planning and taking a tour is the one thing that, in my opinion, will most nearly insure *growth* in every way. It will bring more people to the music program, pull them together and change their lives (and yours) for the better faster than any other kind of project I know about. We've discovered many ways to put a tour together. Here are some ideas that may help you have a successful experience.

I can't take for granted that your group is so good musically that that's the reason you want to take them out on the road, so let me say it is important in my opinion to strive for excellence in your musicianship. Nobody said you have to be *great* in order to go—but if the quality of your presentation doesn't demand people's attention, you have no business wasting their time. And when I consider representing Jesus Christ, I feel strongly that if the quality of my program turns people away and embarrasses the group and me—better we stayed at home and practiced!

Planning the Program

What to practice: choosing the right music for a group is critical. Today there is a lot of great material from which to choose. If I am working with a group which is relatively inexperienced, I try to choose music that will be easy enough to give them early success. As we go along I add more difficult things to keep them challenged. And even when I have been caught in the "special number for the evening service" routine, I have used those same numbers for the tour at the end of the year.

"In the beginning the choir director chose the music, after much looking, much thought and careful planning!" So begins the creation of a touring music group. When I am organizing a tour for spring, my fall and winter music is the basis for my spring road program. By then I usually know what songs work and those that don't can be replaced.

I believe in variety but within a definite unifying theme. Recently the Continentals did a concert based on the theme, "Light," using the musical *And There Was Light!* as the basis. The program was designed to last ninety minutes. Other years we have used subjects like: Praise *(Come Praise and Bless The Lord),* and Love *(Sing It with Love).*

Having a direction to my program is for me essential. I want people to go away knowing what was said to them. The theme may be subtle or it may be very open and direct, but for each tour I have a theme with a definite direction. Every number needs to be good enough to stand on its own. That way the choir can use them as "specials" throughout the year as well as in the tour program.

If our program is all one style, people quickly become bored with it. For the group's sake and the audience's, I plan plenty of variety. In planning for a tour where many different audiences and age levels are involved, here are some styles that we often include in our program: contemporary Christian songs and arrangements; hymns; spirituals; anthems; festival anthems; scripture songs; fun songs; a production number or something dramatic from a musical; a band only number (if I take instrumentalists along); gospel songs from various periods of Christian music; arrangements of old and new songs in various styles from a cappella to disco, with or without choreography; and the list goes on.

Here is a formula for an average tour concert program in three parts:

PART ONE

Opening: An up tempo attention-getter that usually sets the theme. Might be old or new, but definitely rhythmic and exciting!

Next: Continue with something familiar. Perhaps a medley where you may be relatively sure everybody can relate to a song they know. You are trying to win the approval of the audience here.

Down and Pretty: Describes the third ingredient. This one is to settle the crowd and should be a selection which can minister through the lyrics.

Change of Pace: May be an arrangement for the children—a fun song with choreography or even a spiritual with lots of movement.

Moving On: Something which will bridge to a more serious song, like a contemporary arrangement of a popular gospel song.

Heavier: But not the climactic moment yet. Now the music begins to get more serious. Perhaps a production number or festival anthem, a patriotic song, or anything that will lead toward the theme and leave the audience inspired.

PART TWO

Now change pace to keep people's attention. Perhaps a solo, duet, trio or some other ingredient that lies within the group, to give the audience versatility but still quality while the rest of the group makes a visual change by sitting, or leaving to either change clothes or simply take a break.

PART THREE

The last part of the program is directed toward the theme and is definitely more serious.

Building: To build toward the high point, use three or four songs, or part of a musical broken up with testimony and sharing from a few members of the choir.

High Point: For the climactic moment musically, use a "chiller"—something that moves people both with lyrics and musical inspiration.

Transition: Then follow it up with an opposite—a quiet, introspective song and arrangement that will emotionally touch someone.

Closing: From there the program can be closed with some type of spiritual music, and after the point is made, close with a finale number that restates the theme.

After I have selected the program, I then set ten months aside to plan the itinerary, the promotion, the finances, the outfits, the equipment, the transportation and the rules of behavior.

Where to Go

To have a tour, we need a geographical turnaround point for the trip. The distance we can travel to a destination is determined by the length of time the group can be away. If our tour is all summer, we can go anywhere there are people, but if it's over an Easter holiday week and we only have eight days, we can only go as far as we can comfortably bus in four days. That would be an absolute maximum of 1,200–1,400 miles in one direction. Considering what the cost may be ($2.00 per mile or more by the time all bills are paid) I sometimes want to stay even closer to home than that!

Three hundred miles (8 to 10 hours) in one day is a long bus day, but we do that a lot! Two hundred miles (5 to 6 hours) is much more comfortable. For a first tour, I recommend that you stay closer to home—maybe a neighboring state or some nearby scenic tourist spot, doing concerts on the way and back, choosing a different route each way.

Booking an Itinerary

Now that the geographical turnaround point has been chosen, the next step is to find churches to serve as hosts along the way. This is where I found out that to be a good tour director you have to be a salesman, too, and a promoter, and a spiritual leader, and an emcee, and a . . . it's a big job! But if you like work, you'll love setting up a tour.

Who wants to hear our group? Well, I usually begin by deciding what our objective is. Are we going to sing to Christians, non-Christians, old or young, foreign or domestic, Baptist or Pentecostals, or all of the above? It makes a difference!

For your first few tours, I suggest making it easy on yourself. Go to churches where there are people you know, or at least churches in your own denomination. Believe me, in today's world of more groups than churches, you *need* an "in"! Booking cold is a lost cause. Your letter may not even be answered. The truth is that most churches get many, many more requests than they can possibly entertain, so if it's a short tour, give the church contact a call. If we are going out for 8 weeks and 56 concerts, I start a year ahead and begin by first sending out letters to churches along our tentative route.

If you book by mail (few people do successfully) there are some basic questions a prospective host will have. These can be answered in a "Host Responsibility Information Sheet," which should be included with your letter. At the end of this chapter, I have included one that the Continental Singers have used successfully for many years.

In addition to the letter and information sheet, I send a copy of our previous summer's program to give the sponsor an idea of our music. If you have not done a tour before, then I suggest that you write up a description of your proposed program and send it with your cover letter and the Host Info Sheet.

In the cover letter I basically describe who we are, what we do, when we'd like to come, and why a church should accept us. We send out a "Continental Fact Sheet" on which we have written about a paragraph on each of these headings:

Who Are We?
What's Our Program Like?
Where Are We Going?
What Do Pastors and Laymen Say about the Continentals?
Other Churches Who've Sponsored Us

If you've been on the road before, these kinds of things make the prospective hosts aware that you're experienced. If you haven't, then substitute some information about the group and the goals of the group—perhaps about why you're going on this tour, or other outreach projects you've done together before this tour.

Sixty days later, if I haven't received a response, I send a reminder letter or postcard. If I haven't heard thirty days after that, I write to a new contact. At some point I finish the arrangements on the phone with the parties who respond.

Most hosts need at least sixty days to promote your concert in order to have an audience. So sixty days from an "open" date on your itinerary—go ahead and panic!!!

Promotion

Promotion is helpful if you want people to find out about your concert. Sundays and Wednesdays are easy in many churches, as the crowd is built in and the church staff has done its announcing. But Monday, Tuesday, Thursday, Friday and Saturday are tough. If it's a short tour, I consider it a waste of money to print posters and flyers. I recommend having an artist in your church make up a dozen or so posters for you on which you can glue an 8″ × 10″ picture of the group.

If you are going to be on tour for the summer, print! A standard 8½″ × 11″ flyer is a very effective promotion piece. On the front of the flyer you might put a picture and the group's name. On the back put a description of your program and a few quotes from music people and pastors who have heard it and liked it. Using colored paper to print on also makes the flyer more eye-catching.

For newspapers, send the host a black and white glossy picture of yourself and/or the group with biographical information, and a write-up about the group and where they are going. Include a description of the program. If there is anything newsworthy about you or anyone in the group, be sure to include it too! *

You can get really exotic with your promotion, but because of today's costs, I recommend keeping it clean and simple. A dollar is hard to get back, especially if the offering at the concert doesn't even pay for the bus mileage that day getting to the concert. If you traveled 300 miles at $2.00 per mile, that's $600! How often do you take a $600 offering? I can tell you my average is hundreds lower. That's why I urge you not to depend totally on offerings for your income.

*Finances***

When you make out your budget, I suggest that you check with the church or music department to see if they are willing to make up the difference between your expenses and the offerings you will receive. If they are not able to help, then each person in the group could be responsible to raise a sponsorship amount equal to the total budget divided by the number of people going on tour. The first tour I ever took, the kids raised $75 each for the five weeks. Today the figure is much, much larger.

Outfits

Let's say you get your eight days booked and promoted and you have a program well into rehearsal—good show! You still have ninety days to find outfits, that is, if you like outfits. I do, but then I'm a product of the Sixties.

For kids, forget the robes on the one end and jeans and cutoffs on the other, and settle for something "clean-cut" in the middle!

We usually pick out a pattern or two for the girls—they can make theirs. The boys are the problem, so we pick out the boys' outfits *first* and match the girls to it. For church groups, we usually

---

* Chapter 15 has more details about how to write a news story and other details about promotion.

** Chapter 3 has more ideas about ways to raise money for special projects.

end up at Ward's or Sears for the boys, or a good men's store that can provide twenty of the same blazers.

Versatility is the key. The right blazer with two pairs of pants (a matching pair and a contrasting pair) and a long tie and bow tie, informal shirt which can be worn with the long tie or open, and dress shirt which can be worn with the bow tie or long tie, can be both a formal tux and a sports coat. It's worked for us for seventeen years, and it saves the kids money, too.

Without a doubt, of all the various details associated with touring, the outfit problems—getting material, shoes that match, the coat for the late recruit, and so on—are the toughest, nastiest and least desirable part of the whole thing! Experience speaks! Believe it—and start looking in plenty of time.

Equipment

For sound, I suggest getting a good portable Shure system with BOSE speakers and an SM58 Shure microphone for each riser. We use SR101 mixers and 300 watt Crown amps, but there are less expensive ways to do it.

I recommend Sound Investment Enterprises, P. O. Box 4139, Thousand Oaks, California, 91359, for more detailed help. They have been outfitting us for years at reasonable prices. I get no commission, but I promise they can help you.

I would not recommend that you invest in lights unless touring is to be a big deal for your group. For short tours now and then, I recommend that you rent lighting. You might want to buy a spotlight. I use Trooperettes, and they cost about $1,000 each.

I've found that building boxes for all our travel equipment has helped it last a long time. For us it is essential. I could give you sizes and designs, but you might not buy what we use. So I suggest finding a carpenter in your church and having some of your own boxes specially built.

We use fiber glass risers of our own design, but I think you will be just fine with standard school-choir risers purchased from a music dealer or borrowed from a high school. And if there are twelve singers or less, I don't think you need risers at all.

Buses: Charter vs. Lease

For the first tour . . . keep it simple. If you have a good church bus, I would use it. But if it's not a GMC Diesel, don't go too far! Most often, tour groups either charter or lease, and there is a difference.

The charter will cost more money, but has less headaches. Many companies will not lease, and so you may have to charter. Some companies cannot go out of state, so if you are going beyond your state line, be sure to ask that question early. With a charter you must use the company's driver. The cost will include a per-day charge, plus mileage or a *larger* per day fee without mileage. Don't be surprised if it costs $500 a day!

The charter cost includes gas, fees, repairs and maintenance, insurance, driver, and his expenses. The nice thing about a charter is that if the bus breaks down, it is the bus company's responsibility to get you another bus immediately and at their expense. And believe me, buses do break down, no matter how new they might be.

A lease, on the other hand, is just like owning the bus! You use your own driver, pay your own gas, road fees, maintenance, and (worst of all) repairs! And bus repairs aren't cheap! However, if you have an experienced diesel bus (not school bus) driver in your congregation and a good bus leasing company that will provide the insurance, then leasing is much less expensive.

Not all buses are the same. I would never lease a 4501 scenic-cruiser. GMC 4104s, 4106s and 4107s are fine for 35–39 people, but if you take that many you'll also need a van for equipment and hang-up bags. The new MC7s, MC8s and GMC 4903 and GMC 4905 types are fantastic, but really expensive. Because bus companies have to wait up to two years to get one, they are not likely to lease one to you. For a number of years now I have leased GMC 4106s exclusively. It's a great bus. As for the equipment van, I use Ford vans, but any good, *heavy-duty* van will do.

Travel Discipline

When you get it all together and "go on the road," travel discipline is critical. I try to keep the group spiritually directed. I've noticed that often attitudes on the bus are carried over into the concert, so I am particular about what I allow the kids to wear (no cutoffs or jeans on the bus), or what they listen to (no radios or tape decks for one whole week!). I also prepare a discipline study program for the tour.

For the length of the tour these kids are 100 percent mine. Everyone is always there. Nobody misses rehearsal or a prayer time. It's wonderful! I try to take advantage of it and make it count for the spiritual growth of each person. To me, that's what it's really all about!

Products and By-Products

Almost all Christian tours have as their ultimate goal the spiritual growth of the people on the tour *and* the ministry to the audiences. You hope there will be some non-Christians who will hear the gospel message, and Christians who will be challenged and inspired. By-products include audience entertainment, group unity, travel and the pure spiritual growth of the leaders—you and me. I am often surprised at myself. I am often the person who grows the most, gains the most, and loves it the most—and so can you. Because in order to be successful, I believe you will have to be the one to give the most. The biblical principle is clear. . . .

It gives me greater security when I am organized and plan carefully in advance. I try to have alternate plans, too, because it seems that if something can go wrong, it probably will. If it sounds like too much work, remember (as I often do!): "To whom much is given, much is required." If you get discouraged (count on it), "Seek first the kingdom of God and all these things will be added unto you." It's not your (or my) program or tour in the final analysis after all.

And finally, honor the audience with a quality performance, one with variety, good pacing and a spiritually directed theme clear enough that everyone knows why your group came and what was said.

Music is a wonderful vehicle for the gospel. When you hit the road to present it to others, wrap it in a beautiful package!

About the Contributor: *Cam Floria, president of Continental Singers which sends multiple choirs on the road all over the world each summer, has developed some practical procedures contained in this chapter. It is designed for your first tour, or for subsequent ones, whether or not the early ones seemed like the next thing to total disaster.*

With a B. Mus. Ed. degree from Northwestern College and an M. Mus. Ed. degree from Lewis & Clark College, Cam has worked in the field of Christian music, helping to create innovative ways to spread God's Word and the news of his love. Cam has been president of Continental Singers since 1967, and has also been president of Christian Artists' Corporation since 1974. His building these two organizations has certainly shown his abilities in musicianship, organization, dedication and stamina. In addition, he has composed and arranged many choral collections and musicals which have been published by Lexicon Music and National Music Service (a division of N.L. Records and C.A. Music). Other interests include tennis and scuba diving. Cam and his wife, Cher, live in Thousand Oaks, California.

CONTINENTAL SINGERS AND ORCHESTRA
HOST INFORMATION
SUMMER—1980

Please read the material on the sheet carefully. By accepting a Continental concert, you agree in general to meet the obligations listed here. These procedures may need to be adjusted to fit your situation. The information is designed to answer most of the questions usually asked about concert details, but subsequent correspondence will clarify any changes.

( ) HOUSING (for evening hosts)
There will be approximately 22 boys, 18 girls and one married couple to house for one night. The exact number will be known about 30 days prior to the concert. Because of the equipment loading problem, hosts will need to wait about 30 minutes after the program before individual members of the group can leave for the homes. By the way, it's not possible for us to provide bedding (sleeping bags, etc.).
NOTE: Continental Small Group Outreach will have approximately 13 boys, 10 girls, and one married couple to house.

( ) MEALS
Evening Hosts: It's really important for the young people for sponsors to provide a HOT meal at the church, in homes, or at a nearby restaurant, at least two hours before the concert (2½ hours if in homes). Please let us know if you plan to have them go to the homes for dinner to coordinate arrival and car pick-up times.
Overnight host families will need to provide a BREAKFAST in the home and a SACK LUNCH.

Sunday A.M. Hosts: The sponsor is asked to provide the noon meal at the church or in a nearby restaurant, unless otherwise notified.

( ) FINANCIAL INFORMATION
Financial matters are very important to the maintenance of the Continental ministry. We prefer to come on a freewill offering basis without a specific guarantee. (It might be helpful for you to know that our average daily expenses are $____.*)

( ) PROMOTION
News releases, photos, radio spots, TV slides and spots, promotional record albums, posters and flyers (or inserts for mailing and church bulletins) are available in any quantity to promote the concert.

( ) PIANO REQUIREMENTS
We need to have one piano, tuned to the standard A-440, not longer than a day or two before the concert program, if at all possible. This is vital for a quality program for you.

( ) PLATFORM—TECHNICAL REQUIREMENTS—USHERS
(A) Platform furniture will need to be removed to accommodate our risers and singers (except for short Sunday morning performances). Please let us know in advance if this presents any problems for you.
(B) Electrical requirements:
1) We use our own sound and lighting equipment and carry our own crew to handle them. Our spotlight, sound equipment, and

* Fill in your own amount after planning your budget.

musical instruments will operate on your regular 110 volt circuits. 2) For our fixed lighting, we need a form of 220 volt current. Because the correct 220 current is often not available, we have designed a system to "create" it by hooking into a normal circuit breaker panel. No special arrangements are necessary, unless the procedure above is not permissible. In that event, please contact our office for detailed instructions.

(C) Please provide ushers to distribute Continental programs (supplied to you without cost) before the concert and to receive the offering during the program.

(D) We will need 10 folding chairs for the orchestra accompanying the Continental Singers. Continental Brass requires 20 chairs.

( ) OUTDOOR CONCERT—SPECIAL "ADDITIONAL" REQUIREMENTS *

(A) Two clean dressing rooms within 200 feet of the stage for 20 people each (with luggage), plus conveniently located bathrooms.

(B) Stage elevated at least 2 feet and at least 30 feet long by 15 feet deep.

(C) Enough 110 volt current to carry a maximum load of 80 amps.

(D) In case of rain, alternate facilities are necessary—we must protect technical equipment from the slightest amount of moisture.

* All other needs mentioned on this sheet are still effective.

( ) CONCLUSION

Every concert is planned to have a lasting spiritual impact on the listener. Closing comments may be handled by our tour director or the local sponsor.

Andrea (Noni) Wells Miller

15.

Publicity Basics: Covering the Bases

From the editor: *One rainy night I attended a concert in a small church on the outskirts of our city—only because I had happened to overhear two people talking about it at the office. The concert was marvelous, presented by a small group of talented, committed Christian kids who had decided to give a year of their lives to traveling and sharing the gospel through music. I laughed with them as they lovingly satirized some familiar shortcomings of us Christians. I cried as their music moved me closer to Jesus Christ. And I ached inside when I looked around the sanctuary to see only 15 or 20 people who had braved the stormy weather to participate in this experience.*

The performers sang as if there were a packed house, yet I couldn't keep myself from wondering how they did it with the reality of the empty pews staring back at them. And I thought, Why didn't somebody get the word out about this fantastic concert?!

On many occasions, relying only on announcements made in Sunday school or church and printed in the bulletin and weekly newsletter is just not enough. Of course, we can't widely publicize every single meeting and event sponsored by the church, yet when special concerts or guest musicians come to town and we want to reach beyond our church doors, it seems that more effective kinds of promotion are needed.

I have become aware that a feeling of excitement is added to an event when a "publicity campaign" is carried out. People seem to think, "If this concert is important enough for all these posters, letters in the mail, radio announcements and newspaper stories, then it's probably something I shouldn't miss." And publicity can also do a lot for the morale of the singers and others involved in the performance when they see their names and faces in print!

This chapter includes a few basic ideas I have used in my work in marketing at Word, and these can serve as a starting point from which you can build your own specially designed campaign. I hope that by using some of them, you'll notice a difference in the size of the congregation the night or nights you perform.

During the time I was Marketing Director for Music for Word, Inc., I learned, through talking to music ministers, that ministry has basically two parts: (1) having something God wants us to say and preparing ourselves to say it, and (2) finding the people to whom God wants us to communicate. After all the months of rehearsals and preparation, the members of the choir have probably felt a certain amount of ministry among themselves. They may have experienced this through studying the lyrics of the music, through the fellowship and contact with each other and their director, and through the fulfillment of their own musical gifts from God and the returning of those gifts to him. Yet, no matter how rigorous the rehearsals, how perfect the performance, how elegant the costumes, how powerful the message or how exciting the music, if the right audience isn't there to experience it, then it seems to me a major part of the purpose of ministry is missing.

At Word I was "Music Ombudsperson," a title I invented for around the office, which meant that I was someone who was the "go-between" for two groups of people: those who compose music and those who perform it. It was my role to communicate back and forth to each group about the needs of the other. In the process I developed some publicity basics which I believe can be applied to letting a church congregation and the community at large know that a musical event is going to happen—and motivating people to attend!

The first phase of a publicity campaign is the planning. I suggest that you plan the promotion schedule and budget, which I will discuss later in this chapter, at the same time you plan the rehearsal schedule. In the very beginning, it is helpful to select someone whom you can depend on to be the "Publicity Manager." After planning the promotion schedule and budget together, you should be able to rely on this person to carry out the publicity details. The person might be a member of the choir, or someone who is not involved musically but wants to participate. Go over the ideas you have concerning publicity and budget with that person, and you may want to give him or her this chapter to read. Make sure he or she understands the financial limitations . . . then turn loose! An occasional checking-in meeting between the two of you is a good idea. It keeps you informed and relaxed about the fact that the plan is being carried out, and it lets the Publicity Manager know that his or her work is a vital part of the ministry and that you care about how it is carried out!

The rest of this chapter is addressed specifically to the person in charge of the publicity . . . whoever that is.

Publicity Which Costs Little or No Money

The publicity tactics can be divided into two categories: those which cost money and those which don't. I am aware that nothing is really free, that even things which don't cost money cost something . . . time, effort, discipline, dedication, sense of purpose. But for the next few pages, I will use money as the basic dividing line for these two categories.

News Releases

A news release is perhaps one of the most effective types of communication and costs little or nothing. It's a good idea to call your local newspaper to ask what the deadlines are for news stories, what length limitations there are, if any, and also if the newspaper would be interested in sending a reporter and a photographer to a rehearsal to write his or her own story. Sometimes the religious editor, entertainment editor or community interest editor might be looking for an idea for a story. It is the Publicity Manager's responsibility to set up the appointment after making sure the music director is available, greet the reporter and photographer when they show up and act as host or hostess while they are there, answering any questions and arranging any interviews that might be desired.

If it turns out that no one from the paper will write a story, you will need to do the writing yourself. But don't despair. There is a fairly simple formula which I will describe in some detail here. And even if the newspaper decides to write up a story about your performance, it is still up to you to prepare and send news releases to the regional and state denominational papers as well as to the church newsletter.

How to Begin

The first news release should be worded as an announcement, informing the public that the plans and rehearsals for your event are now under way. I usually send news release announcements to city newspapers three to four weeks before the first performance.

Following the announcement, different reminder stories can be written and sent to the same papers each week until the final week of the performance, then daily, or at least three times during the performance week itself.

Content

When composing your news story, try to put the answers to these five basic questions all in the first paragraph: who, what, where, when, why. Also, this paragraph should be no more than five or six lines. In case the editor has a full paper and only has space for a short story, he or she can easily lift out this first paragraph, and it will have complete information.

The rest of the paragraphs can enlarge on the basic story. Each paragraph should be placed in order of importance, with the last paragraph being the least important. If the editor has to cut, he or she will probably remove the last paragraph, and so on until the story fits.

When choosing your words, try to aim the story at the general public, not at musicians, and at a reading level of about the third grade. Granted, most people read at a higher level than this, but when scanning a newspaper, people often remember what your story said if it is worded simply and can be quickly and easily read. Avoid technical musical terms or "churchy" terms. Choose simple synonyms for these terms, even if it means using several short words in place of one long one. For example, instead of saying, "The first act closes with a beautiful a cappella rendition of 'God Bless America,' " you might say, "The first act closes with the choir singing alone, without music from the organ, a beautiful setting of the hymn 'God Bless America.' "

Also, since space is limited and you are working for a simple story, stick to the facts. Try not to exaggerate or use emotional phrases to describe your performance. Rather than saying, "The outstanding F.B.C. high school choir will enthusiastically perform a hysterical musical comedy guaranteed to lift your spirits and brighten your day," a simple statement like "The high school choir of First Baptist Church will present the Musical comedy, 'Nicodemus Up a Tree' on a Friday, April 12, 1980, at 8:00 P.M. in the sanctuary of the church," will be much more effective.

Now that you have all these guidelines in mind, it might be difficult to start writing. A favorite technique of mine is to sit down with a blank piece of paper and pretend I am *telling* someone about this event. After saying it outloud, I write it down. Then after I have all the information on paper, I go back over what I've written and polish it, keeping all the suggestions above in mind. I use my usual vocabulary at first, then go back, pick out the longer words and technical terms and substitute smaller ones. This "talking it through first" has saved me endless hours of agony spent staring at a blank piece of paper with an equally blank mind, trying to write a brochure or news story about a workshop, concert or new musical.

Form

A news release should be sent to the newspaper typewritten, double spaced on one side of 8½″ by 11″ sheets of paper. Leave at least a one inch margin on each side and start typing one third of the way down the first page.

In the upper right hand corner of the top sheet, be sure to indicate the release date. If there is no specific date, just put "For Immediate Release" on the page. In the opposite corner, list your name and telephone number, in case the editor at the paper has any questions and needs to contact someone.

Try to keep the headline as brief as possible. For me, the maximum length is one line, and I can usually get it down to five or six words, which is even better! Otherwise, I run the risk of having a news editor re-do my headline and who knows what may appear in the paper!

If the story is longer than one page, type "MORE" at the center of the bottom of the first page, so the editor will be aware that it goes on to other pages, in case the pages become separated in the typeset room. On the last page (or at the bottom of the first page if it is a one page story), indicate that the story has ended with one of these: ###, –30, or ****. This assures the typesetter that he or she has indeed reached the end of the story.

Pictures

It usually increases the interest level of stories when pictures are sent with them. Action pictures are much more eyecatching than the traditional "mug shot" or head and shoulders portrait we see so often in newspapers. To announce the beginning of a church musical event, you might get a picture of the director, accompanist and leading characters grouped around a piano going over a song. For follow-up stories, try for action, such as members of the set crew hammering on a piece of the set, or actors going through their blocking rehearsals, or leading characters in costume.

Newspaper editors prefer pictures which are at least 5″ x 7″, black and white, glossy. I write the captions myself, making sure to identify everyone in the picture and describe what they are doing. I try to do this in one sentence if possible, two as a maximum. This is typed on a piece of paper a little larger than the picture, then attached at the bottom of the picture with tape on the *back* side (Never put tape on the front of a picture). I then fold the paper up over the print to protect the surface.

When sending pictures with a news story, never attach the picture to the story. Paper clips and staples can damage the surface of the photograph. The best way I have found to keep the picture and story together is to fold the story in half, slip the picture inside this fold and put the entire packet into a 5″ x 7″ envelope to deliver it to the paper. If you mail the envelope, also insert a piece of cardboard to protect the picture from getting bent.

If you want the picture returned, indicate that on the back, including your name and address. Never use a ball point pen or a typewriter on the back of a picture. Both of these make crease marks on the front which ruin it for printing. I often use a felt tip pen and do not press hard. When doing this I make sure that I have blotted the ink and let it dry thoroughly before it comes in contact with other pictures or papers, so the ink won't rub off.

"Community Calendars"

Many radio stations have an announcement period each day to tell listeners about local events such as art shows, concerts, seminars and group meetings. In my home town it was called the "Community Calendar," though it may have another name in other towns. It is certainly worth phone calls to each radio station to let them know about your concert. (There will be more about paid radio advertising later in this chapter.) Newspapers often have lists like this, too.

Informing the Congregation

The weekly (or monthly) church newsletter is one of the basic places in which to publicize the concert. Instead of relying on the usual editor of the newsletter to write up the news of your concert, take the time to write an interesting story yourself. Check with the regular editor to see how much space is available and when the deadline is. Try to put a catchy headline on your story to get the attention of the newsletter scanners who breeze through the paper each week (or month).

The church bulletin is another basic source of information for the congregation. A brief statement each week will keep the date of the concert in their minds.

Asking all the Sunday school department leaders to add an announcement about the concert to their announcements can also increase congregational awareness.

Publicity Which Costs Money

Some other aspects of a publicity campaign which *do* cost money include posters, radio advertising, newspaper advertising, billboards, mailings, T-shirts and other eye-catching gimmicks. How many of these you will be able to do will depend on the money available in the budget.

The first thing I do is daydream about all the possibilities, make a list, then check on the costs for each item. From this itemized list, I can then choose various ideas and put together a campaign that has interest and still stays within the budget limits I know I must keep.

Posters

Posters can range in type from simple hand-made sheets to full-color, printed ones and costs vary accordingly. If you are or know of any talented poster makers, before contacting them, think about where you would place the posters so you'll know how many you need. Then go window shopping to find out how much the materials will cost, if they are not already available in the regular church supply room. Add these costs to your daydream list.

Many music publishers provide printed posters that match the artwork on the cover of the musical you may be performing. The posters often come in sets of twenty-five or so, and it is well worth a call, or if you have time, a letter to the publisher to find out if such posters are available and how much they cost. They usually have blank spaces at the bottom in which to fill in the details about your specific performances.

Once the posters are made or purchased, effective placement is the next thing to plan. Strategic points around the church, in local high schools, in the businesses of church members, in public places like laundromats, car washes, and so on are often effective.

Brainstorm with choir members to find out who owns businesses (or works for major companies in town where many local people come and go). Ask these people if you can bring them a poster (or posters) to put up. Then deliver the posters yourself or delegate a sensitive member of your group to help you if you are placing dozens or hundreds of posters. Since the business people are doing you a favor by granting you free advertising space, I believe you should do the work necessary and be sure to thank the appropriate people for their help. I have found that it is most effective to make an appointment to meet the person in charge at their business with the poster and decide then where to put it up. If you just give them posters at church or drop them by their homes, even though they have good intentions, "forgetfulness" can strike and the poster might never be placed in the best location to be seen by the people passing by. It is the Publicity Manager who has the goal of promoting the concert, so it is important that he or she be motivated to get the poster to its final destination.

Radio Advertising

Another possibility is radio advertising. Each radio station has its own advertising rates, so it's worth a call to each one for information. Also ask about how to have an advertisement made. They have people who will help you put together an ad, including professional D.J. voices and copy writers. There is a standard of quality which each ad must meet, so just any old tape recorded message probably won't measure up. The people at the station can give you information about cost and good procedures. Take this information down for your daydream list when planning the budget, including the *name* of the person at the station you would work with if you decided to do radio advertising. Then, you'll be able to talk to the same person again.

Newspaper Advertising

Newspaper ads are also effective. I try to get my ads on the entertainment page with the movies and restaurants. I believe that page is read more than almost any other page in the paper. If I can't get the ad on this page, then the religious page with the church listings might reach part of my audience. Each newspaper has different deadlines and rates for different sized ads, so I suggest you call all the papers in your town.

The content and layout of the ad is important for effectiveness. To me, the most important point to remember is to keep it as uncluttered as possible. Perhaps the name of your program, the place, time, date and location, and any prominent soloist(s) whose name(s) might draw interested people, are all that you need to include.

A Musical

HERE COMES THE SON!

Presented by

THE CELEBRATION SINGERS

May 3, 4, 5, 1980	Memorial Presbyterian
8:00 P.M.	100 S. Hope Street
Free Admission	Arlington

For Reservations, call 999–0000 8:30 A.M.–4:30 P.M.

Billboards

Portable billboards that can be rented are eye-catching and popular. Add the cost of renting a few of these to place on church grounds or at various places around town to your daydream list.

Local businesses such as banks and fast food restaurants sometimes have billboards available for community news. There is often little or no charge for these.

Some people have been able to get signs placed on city buses and taxi cabs also. There is a charge for this which will vary from city to city, so again a telephone call is necessary.

Mailings

Mailings are an effective way to reach people if what you mail them is creative—not just another piece of "junk mail." Since your church probably sends out a newsletter to its members every week or month, the church can provide you with the mailing labels to the church members. Or they might let you insert a mailing piece with the bulletin by paying only the added mailing cost.

What to Mail

A quick postcard with the basic information is one way to reach the church membership. Or sometimes a more elaborate letter from the senior minister, the minister of music and/or the music committee is more appropriate.

Publishers provide a miniature version of the poster I mentioned earlier, called a handbill, which can be mailed with a letter. It has the same small blank space at the bottom on which you can put information about your performance dates and times. These handbills can also be used inside the church bulletin each Sunday for several weeks before the concert.

A self-mailer is a printed sheet of paper, folded, addressed, and mailed without an envelope. This form eliminates the cost of envelopes and can be a very effective way to mail.

Even if you're not charging an admission fee, a very strong incentive for people to attend a concert is to receive admission tickets. Somehow having a ticket to a program often makes one much more likely to remember it and attend. If you print up tickets, give the name, date, time and location of the concert and encourage people to keep them in their billfolds to remind them of the event.

Postage Rates

If your church has a nonprofit organization mailing permit, you can have the permit printed on your mailing, too. This is the least expensive kind of postage rate. If the church does not have such a permit, then check with the post office about getting a bulk rate permit. If you are mailing 200 or more identical pieces, zip coded, then you can benefit from this bulk rate. The permit costs about $40 per year at this time, but if you are going to mail more than once a year, this still is a great savings from regular first class postage.

When to Mail

A mailing should be sent to the church membership at least five weeks before the event if it is being sent bulk rate. I have found that it often takes up to three weeks for delivery of bulk rate pieces, although in some cases part of the mailing may arrive within a week! If it's a first class mailing, then it can be sent about three weeks early, allowing a week for delivery. If it's mailed any earlier, I've noticed that people tend to forget about the event. If the mailing is sent any later, the letters sometimes don't arrive until after the program, or too close to the actual date for people to make plans, arrange for babysitters and so on.

T-Shirts

T-shirts are popular today, and many T-shirt companies can print photographs and other things on the shirts. I recommend investigating the cost of ordering a batch of shirts for the choir members to wear with the name of the musical as it is shown in the art work from the music books. Each choir member could buy one and wear it around during the rehearsal weeks, helping to let people know that the performance is going to take place.

Eye-Catching Gimmicks

While this phrase may sound a little "carnival" for your taste, it best describes the kind of attention-getters that can help people remember the event you are motivating them to attend. One year when Kurt Kaiser's musical "Just for You" was being premiered, I felt that the title had so many possible meanings, that I wanted to find a way to help the choir directors who attended a Word workshop to be aware of this musical and be motivated to attend the premiere. I wanted to find a way to put that title, "Just for You," in front of them daily in a repetitive way that was not bothersome. The result: notepads with the lettering from the art work for the musical across the top. Imagine the impact of getting a note which, instead of being "A Note from *ME,*" was a note "Just for *You.*"

I am still using the few notepads I have left, but this illustrates the kind of eye-catcher that you can dream up. Perhaps a bookmark or Christmas tree ornament would suit your musical event. The eye-catcher starts out as part of the publicity campaign and ends up being a memento of a marvelous experience!

Daydream and make a list of all the possibilities you can with a committee. Make telephone calls or shopping trips to get an estimate of the costs involved. Then refine the list to include the things you have money for, schedule the various procedures (picture sessions, writing, getting items to printers, and so on) and carry them out. An effective publicity campaign is one of the many tools we have with which to go into all the world and tell the people about God's love and redemption.

About the Contributor: *Andrea (Noni) Wells Miller has a B.A. in Music from Furman University and did graduate study in music theory at Baylor University. In 1970 she began working at Word, Inc., and was eventually Director of Marketing for Music there.*

During the years at Word, she worked in the music order department and later was director of workshops and coordinator of the Choral Music Preview Plan and the Cassette Preview Service (Word Music). Also she organized staged premieres of musicals including "The Gathering," "Festival of Praise," "Just For You," "Breakfast in Galilee," "The Witness" and "Christmas 2001."

At the present time she is a consultant and writer, and has had articles published in "Christian Bookseller," a magazine for book and music store dealers. She has also co-authored with Keith Miller a cassette tape group study course for single people called "Faith, Intimacy and Risk in the Single Life" (Word), and a book, The Single Experience *(Word).*

Other interests are keeping fit by swimming and jogging, photography, writing short stories, studying and experimenting with nutrition, and traveling with her husband, Keith.

The Inside Track on Your Professional Relationships

Lloyd Ogilvie

16.

What Pastors Wish Choir Directors Knew

From the editor: *Have you ever gone home from a staff meeting wondering what the pastor* really *thinks about your role as minister of music and how that relates to his role as pastor? While there is usually some professional discussion about your role when you first met the pastor, how much ongoing dialogue do you have now?*

Whether or not your relationship with your pastor seems to need some attention, I hope this chapter will give you some fresh ideas about how your pastor may view you and your work in relation to him and his.

Lloyd Ogilvie spells out openly in this chapter what he hopes for and strives for in his working relationship with his director of music. Now you can, in the privacy of your own study, peek into the other side of the pastor-minister-of-music relationship and see what is there. It might even be interesting to ask your pastor to read this chapter, and then discuss the places your working relationship corresponds to or differs from the kind of relationship Lloyd strives for.

One of the most vital relationships in a pastor's life is that with his Director of Music. It can maximize his ministry, bring profound satisfaction, and be the source of great encouragement.

I have been privileged to team with outstanding directors throughout my ministry: people like William Whitehead, Ben Bollinger, Douglas Lawrence, and our present director, William Hatcher. Dr. Charles Hirt, Director of Music Emeritus of our church, is an esteemed friend and a consistent source of wisdom and vision in my evolving understanding of music in the life of the church. These men have become trusted companions in the adventure of leading the church. So much of what I want to put to writing here I have learned from them.

The title of this chapter, therefore, may sound presumptuous. These men know what I wish every music director knew. What I have to say is based on what we have hammered out together in the delights and difficulties of planning and leading worship through the years. Also, broad experience in leading clergy conferences throughout the country for two decades has forced me to realize that not all pastors have been as fortunate as I.

Before my mind's eye flash the memories of pastors with whom I have talked deeply about their relationships with their directors of music. In most cases the problem has been that the pastor was not able to clearly articulate his or her goals and vision in a way that could be received without defensiveness. So two tributaries flow into the river of thoughts I want to communicate: the immense growth that I have experienced through the years working with my directors of music, and the longing I have heard from other clergy about how to work more effectively with the man or woman in this strategic position.

There are eight things I want my, and every, director of music to know.

The Church and Worship

The first is my belief about the nature of the church and the central role of worship. To me the church does not exist for itself but for what happens beyond its doors in the world. A congregation is an equipping center for the ministry of the laity. To be in Christ is to be in the ministry. The total program of the local church, to my way of thinking, must be committed to the enabling, equipping and energizing of the people of God.

This is crucial for understanding what I believe is the role of worship and the place of music in it. In worship, I feel the people need to renew their relationship with God, experience healing of their hurts, and be engendered with hope. The sanctuary is neither a lecture hall for the display of the pastor's oratory nor a concert hall for the staging of a musical performance. Rather it is a holy place where the people of God come to be strengthened for their adventure of faith, hope and love in the world. They desperately need God, a moving experience of his grace, and an experience of in-depth fellowship with fellow strugglers.

So often, I have become aware that both the preaching and the music skim over the heads and hearts of worshipers, answering questions they are not asking and offering anthems and responses which do not touch the core of their needs.

Since I feel that we pastors and directors of music are in the process of becoming what we dare to envision, and our leadership of worship will be what we have personally accepted to be the purpose of worship, it is vitally important that we both know and agree to the *why* of worship before arranging the details of the *how* of worship. What does God want to have happen to his people while they are together for worship? What is our boldest dream for what should happen to the minds, emotions, wills, and bodies of those who faithfully gather? Where are the people in all facets of their being as they come, and where, by God's grace, do we feel they should be when they leave? If we could throw caution, preconceptions, customs and traditions to the winds, what would we imagine could happen in the worship life of our congregation?

These are questions I want to ask with my director of music. I have found a freshness, an excitement that is unleashed when, rather than the maintenance of forms of worship, there is bold joint evaluation with freedom to change and expand our horizons.

There are to me irreducible maximums for worship. I expect nothing less than a divine encounter and the healing and liberation of people. I want my director of music to share my belief that all things are possible. Together, I want to claim that our church is living the twenty-ninth chapter in the Book of Acts and that we can expect and claim that exciting things will happen.

With a clear slate and a viable openness, I want to be able to seek out and prayerfully discuss the purpose and boldest vision we can share together. I feel that there is much more creativity and effectiveness in the pastor-director team if together they have gone back to basics, dared to ask the penetrating questions and have come to a mutual understanding and commitment.

Time Together Is a Necessity

That is based on the second thing I want a director of music to know. I want him or her to know that ours is a primary relationship which will demand time together. Our hearts must beat as one. Times of sharing as persons are not a luxury. They are a necessity. A pastor must be vulnerable enough to open himself. Who is the person behind the robe, titles, and authority structure? I want a director of music who knows me as I am, the hopes and the hurts. And I want to know him or her. That takes time—time for fun as well as work, times for sharing and prayer. To me, this relationship is an essential source of affirmation and assurance for both people as human beings, rather than as interdependent performers.

For busy people this requires planning. I have noticed that we do what we think is important. And in my opinion few things except a pastor's family and his own study and prayer are more important than his relationship with his director. I want a director who feels the same commitment. In short, I want him or her to know that I want to be a friend! In the language of Ecclesiastes, I feel that this friendship is a "triple braided cord"—Christ, a director, and a pastor. Three can equal one in mind, heart, purpose, and passion to lead as one voice.

The Adventure of Planning

Next, I want a director of music to share in the adventure of planning. I plan my sermons a year in advance. By August, I know exactly what will be my title, text, and development of every message from the first of September to the end of June. An explanation is written of what the Lord has given me for each service. Then the first draft of the preaching guide is given to the director.

I realize that because of various pressures, all pastors cannot plan this far in advance. And I am grateful for the time I am given each summer to do this planning. But as I finish the year's plan, some of the most enriching times in my ministry are when the director of music and I sit down together for prolonged evaluation of the year's direction and discuss how to be used together to maximize each service around a central theme.

After a time of research of potential music by the director, we meet again to talk over alternative possibilities of how the music he or she has chosen and the message can blend together. This makes it possible to plan everything from the prelude to the postlude for every service. So often the beginning of an idea that has been growing in me is exploded with additional insight and possibilities from the director of music. There is so much which can be done by planning ahead, and I have noticed that a response, an anthem, or a solo which is on target brings a unified flow of thought and inspiration. I often leave these planning sessions so uplifted I want to preach the whole series of messages right then! And my director has told me he feels the surge of power which comes from allowing God to do a new thing through us.

I am very thankful that all of the directors with whom I have worked have shared in evaluating where we are as a congregation and what should be the thrust for each year's content. When the director sees his or her role as being sensitive and aware of the total spiritual life of the congregation and is a praying, planning partner with me as the pastor, we can become confidants and fellow initiators in moving the congregation forward.

The director also brings to the summer planning sessions the major works and programs he would like to do. These are not just music performances. I think of each one as an integral part of the spiritual enrichment of the total church program for the year. Here is where I can become the maximizer for the director's plans as he has been for my preaching plan. This mutual support enables me to publicly affirm, publicize, and interpret to the congregation why each musical work is a strategic opportunity for growth for the congregation.

Planning, to me, should not involve only one year. I want the director, working with the music committee, to develop a ten-year plan. Few things have given our congregation in Hollywood greater freedom and clarity. When we know where God is leading us in the next decade in the total music program, we are able to establish priorities, time lines, and accountability. We know when choirs are to be added, instruments replaced or refurbished, major programs anticipated, tours planned and expansion of music staff provided. The ten-year goals become part of the congregation's strategy for a dynamic decade.

The excellent thing about planning is that it exposes our worship agenda for integration with the total thrust of the parish. I like for the plans for the music department to be drafted by both the music director and me, shared with the staff, refined and accepted by the music committee, and approved by the church officers for presentation to the congregation as a whole.

Communicate—Not Just Impress

Next I want a director of music who is committed to communicating the gospel to people and not just impressing other musicians. I have found it takes a young clergyman about five years to quit preaching to his theological professors and begin speaking to the needs of the people.

It seems to me that the same is often true for directors of music. Whom do they want to please? As long as other directors, the musical experts, and their peers are the focus of security, it seems that they will miss the mark of leading worship which is relevant to where people hurt and provides impetus to new life. When any director or pastor quits thinking about the needs of the people, it is easy to drift into the esoteric.

When the invisible cheering section is made up of musicians with the director of music's point of view, he or she may think he or she is accomplishing God's purpose. Actually, the question to consider, in my opinion, is: Who is setting the pace? Have those people from whom the director of music wants approval grappled with a holistic approach to worship? Have they asked the questions we dealt with above?

Further, I want a director of music who is familiar with and able to lead the choir in the broad spectrum of music including the classical and the popular, the great historic works and the contemporary compositions. If possible, I want both kinds of music in every worship service or a healthy balance in any one month's anthems, responses and solos.

The same should be true of the major programs presented in addition to worship service music. There are classical works and anthems which are great but do not, in my opinion, communicate with people and their needs; and there are contemporary pieces which I think are equally ineffective. I rely on an astute, Spirit-led director with a clear focus on his or her purpose to find works which are uplifting, moving, and impelling from the total spectrum.

I am gratified that the people with whom I have worked do not enjoy the luxury of an attitude I find prevalent among some directors: disdain. I am not a graduate degree student of music, but I have spent my life ministering and preaching to people. I think I know something about what changes people's lives.

There is nothing more disconcerting to me than a director of music of any church where I visit for a preaching mission or at a conference where I speak, who communicates in body language, facial expression, and sometimes words, that he or she is the only judge of what is appropriate and musically "proper." Just as no sane pastor would imply that a musician is not capable of evaluating what is effective in preaching, so too a sensitive musician should try to refrain from that impression about the pastor's knowledge of music. I strongly feel that the two areas must work together.

Now a word about soloists and organists. I think that a solo must minister to people in worship. It is not just a display of vocal range or esoteric nuances. And I also believe that an organist in a service has the souls of hundreds of people at his or her command. She or he prepares the people to meet God afresh and knits the service together—moving people from adoration to confession, to intercession and supplication, to the exposition of the Word, and to the dedication. There are times of reflection, rejoicing, penetration, and triumph. We need thunder and lightning coupled with sensitive meditation. The objective and the subjective must never be wrenched apart.

Further, I want a choir director whose desire to communicate demands articulate choir anthems and solos. While it seems absurd to me to even mention the need for a congregation to hear and understand the words, I have found that it is sometimes difficult to understand some choirs and soloists. There are soloists whose classical training in voice is impressive, and yet, unlike the organist and the instrumentalists, have the wonderful advantage of words. I can't help but ask, "Why not enunciate?"

Lead the Choir Spiritually

The above leads me to my next point. I want a director of music who can lead the choir in becoming a caring, supportive "church in miniature." I rely on him or her to set the pace in helping a choir know why they are participating in leading worship and for whom. I believe nothing can happen *through* us as communicators. We can only reproduce in others what we are in the process of rediscovering in our own lives. Therefore, it seems to me that the spiritual growth of the choir members and soloists is essential to great music in the worship service. The musicians must be open channels of the Spirit's power.

Several things used by other groups in the church can help to make the choir into a profound fellowship. A time of Bible study and prayer before rehearsals sets the mood and purpose. Prayer partners among the choir members can help each person feel cared for. Sharing of needs in the lives of members of the choir enables the whole choir to be a supportive community. I am deeply moved by the way the people in our choirs stand with each other in need and rejoice with each other in times of success and victory.

Our choir elects a chaplain from its members each year. I have listened to these men and women lead devotions and have sensed the profound love of this caring community. Often this love is expressed in specific action all the way from special offerings for crises to appearances as a group at memorial services. The same is true in sharing the joy of weddings, parties, and personal and professional advancement.

This type of sharing, to me, provides the ambience in which a director can rehearse a choir for singing to God's glory. I think that sensitive and insightful explanation of the words and mood of a piece of music results in a more effective rendering of the music in the service. I believe that a choir has an inalienable right to be led by a person who loves God, wants to introduce people to him, and wants a choir to sing to his glory and the edification of a congregation. The results I have seen from this kind of leadership are an intensity and verve which help a choir to sing with depth and joy.

A great preacher had two things put on a plaque on his pulpit. "I preach as a dying man to dying men and women, as if never to preach again." Beneath that were the words of the Greeks who came to inquire about the Lord, "Sir, we wish to see Jesus!" I believe something like this should be placed in the choir rehearsal room, or these words which we have in our clergy robing room on the door through which we must pass to the sanctuary: "Put your arms of love around the congregation." Oh, to be and not to seem!

Cultivate a Choir-Pastor Relationship

Also, to make all this work I think there must be a love relationship between the choir and me. I know that the director can build or block this, for he or she is my primary interpreter with the choir. When the plans, the preaching guide, and music for the year are set, I like for the director to see that every member of the choir has a copy with an inclusive explanation. I believe this helps to make everyone feel a part of a great adventure. Also, a retreat for the choir before the fall season begins is a special time for me to minister to the choir and share my vision as well as my loving gratitude. Great demands are placed on a choir, and I feel it needs affirmation and a feeling of being special.

Know Talents and Gifts

The last thing I want to say is that I need a director of music to know the difference between talents and gifts. He or she and the choir have musical talent, training and experience. I believe leading worship requires the gift of the Holy Spirit. He can take the best we have to offer in our preparation and mysteriously infuse it with his power. Suddenly there is blend, force, and impact.

I believe he has been at work in every worshiper, preparing the way all through the week, and will use the choir, the director and the pastor to fill the emptiness and longing I think people feel to receive power to live the abundant life. When it is all over, it is my desire that we will know that the Lord has used our voices to communicate his love and triumphant adequacy for the many splendored thing we call life.

About the Contributor: *Lloyd Ogilvie holds degrees from Lake Forest College; Garrett Theological Seminary and New College, Faculty of Theology, University of Edinburgh. He has served in Gurnee Community Church, Gurnee, Illinois; Winnetka Presbyterian Church in Winnetka, Illinois; and First Presbyterian Church, Bethlehem, Pennsylvania. He is currently Senior Pastor at First Presbyterian Church of Hollywood, California, where he has been since 1972.*

In addition to preaching, Lloyd appears weekly on his own television program, "Let God Love You!" He is the author of thirteen books, including Drumbeat of Love, When God First Thought of You, Autobiography of God, *and* The Bush Is Still Burning.

A pastor who believes in using the relational approach to the gospel, he stresses four basic relationships in all his preaching, writing and speaking—with God, oneself, others and the world. His sensitivity toward his relationships with God, his family and staff provide a solid background for this approach into the relationship between a pastor and a director of music.

Owen Griffin

17.

What Accompanists Wish Choir Directors Knew

From the editor: One of the key professional relationships you have (or don't have) is with your accompanist. Both in rehearsal and in performance this person can influence the atmosphere for you and the choir—and even the entire congregation.

Here's a chance to look over the shoulder of a professional accompanist for the Billy Graham Crusades as he writes about his own personal experiences with various directors.

One of the things which influences a choral program is the musicianship of the accompanist and his or her attitude toward the relationship with the choir director. I have spent a lot of time "on the bench" in the role of accompanist, but have also known the feeling of being the choir director and working with someone else on the bench. Sometimes while directing, the thought has crossed my mind, *I wonder what he (or she) thought about what I just said?* Then I have remembered a similar situation in a rehearsal in which I have been the accompanist. I have realized that my experience as accompanist has helped me relate to other people when they were in that role with me. So the next few pages will include some of my favorite "choir director habits" as well as a few "pet peeves." Perhaps you're already in touch with some of these things because your accompanist has made you aware . . . painfully or otherwise. But perhaps there'll be something here you can use with your accompanist—

a little something extra that shows you care. I know that when I am accompanying, this can do a lot to improve my attitude in a rehearsal and a performance.

It has been my privilege to serve as accompanist to several outstanding choral directors, from the time I was in junior high school. I have been an accompanist in several churches, and now I am a professional accompanist with the Billy Graham Crusades. Through these years of experience, I have come to appreciate the importance of good communication between the director and the accompanist. As with any art, such communication must be worked at consciously.

Before the Rehearsal

Many problems which could occur in rehearsal can often be eliminated before rehearsal when the director takes the time to discuss with me each new piece of music he or she adds to the repertoire. Most directors with whom I have worked have been considerate enough to give me some time before rehearsal to look at the new music. Of course, I realize this is not always possible. But when it is, the rehearsal is almost certain to run more smoothly.

In one church, I served as music associate and church pianist. I enjoyed my dual role because I had a lot of input into the music program. The director and I made it a practice to study each new piece of music before rehearsal, referring to tempo, dynamics, and other points of interpretation. It also helped a great deal, when time permitted, for him to conduct the entire piece as I played the accompaniment, or the vocal parts if they greatly differed from the accompaniment. This practice saved valuable time in rehearsal and made both of us feel more secure with the music and with each other. I believe that a choir rehearsal should be a rehearsal of the *choir*, not a rehearsal of the conductor or the accompanist.

In that same job, I had the freedom to introduce the director to music he had not heard. As a result, there were many times when I was given the responsibility of deciding which new music would be added to the repertoire. I even had the freedom to disagree with the director on selections or interpretations, but never in front of the choir. I learned to respect his authority on final decisions because he respected my musicianship enough to listen to my suggestions. This balance of respect produced the kind of good working relationship which gave a smooth quality of teamwork to the program.

During Rehearsals

In the rehearsal itself, I prefer that the director be somewhat organized, by listing the music in the order in which he plans to rehearse it. It takes me a little bit of time to find a piece of music in my folder before the director is ready to rehearse. He or she may end up with the score in hand, ready to give the downbeat without realizing the singers and I have not had time to find the music. Calling out a list or writing it on a blackboard at the beginning of rehearsal so I can put the pieces in order before we start can help avoid this delay. Then when it is time to move on to the next piece, a quick glance at me to see if I'm also ready is usually all that needs to be done.

The physical set-up of the rehearsal room can help or hinder the effectiveness of the accompanist. While most directors know that there must be good eye-contact with the singers, it is often easy to forget that the accompanist must also be able to see everything the director does. If the director walks away from the stand to a particular section of the choir with his or her back turned to me, sometimes I can't see the beat. I have actually been accused of not paying attention when in reality I just could not see the beat or hear instructions clearly. I have run into a similar problem when a rehearsal is conducted in an auditorium and the director decides to walk out into the auditorium to check out the acoustics while conducting. Although the choir members have their faces toward him or her, I find myself sitting at a ninety degree angle to the choir *and* the director, and I cannot see my music and the director at the same time.

One of the most common failings I have encountered among choir directors is the tendency to think that somehow I should be able to read the director's mind in rehearsal. While I believe that the accompanist should be alert and attentive to the instructions, I have found that instructions can be very vague at times. For example, I once worked for a director whose instructions frequently referred to the text rather than the page and measure numbers. If he wanted to rehearse a particular passage, he would say, "Go back to 'Alleluia' " (or whatever word or phrase of text it would be). Because there is so much textual repetition in choral music, this rehearsal procedure often is confusing. Although I usually knew which phrase he meant, I could not be sure and neither could the choir. Needless to say, sometimes I would miss altogether. Again, he could have avoided the delay by being more specific.

In a choir where there are more rote-singers than readers the director often depends heavily on me at the piano. I must admit that I do not enjoy playing through each voice part over and over again until the section can sing it. It is boring and mechanical. But when it is necessary to teach by rote, one thing that helps me is for the director to balance the rehearsal with rehearsing some of the music all the way through, relying on the singers who can read music, and also on the leadership I can provide with the piano. This helps keep me from becoming quite so bored and can sometimes provide a greater challenge to those nonreaders to work at sight-reading.

To help reduce this kind of rehearsing, I am willing to spend some time with the director outside rehearsal teaching the nonreaders a little ear-training and sight-singing. I have found that this benefits teacher and student alike.

The director and accompanist really serve as a team in rehearsal. There are times in rehearsal when I play the vocal parts "open score," and as a result, I have learned to think vocally as well as instrumentally. I often hear missed parts which the director does not hear because of his or her giving attention to so many things at one time. If I should mention mistakes to him, I am doing so with the intention of being of help and not to compete with or threaten his or her musicianship or leadership. This, of course, is a lot easier to do with an experienced and secure director, or one whom I know well. And I know that the response from the director depends a lot on what kind of day he or she has had before the rehearsal. I believe the accompanists should try to be sensitive to the feelings of the director in cases like this, but I also hope that the director will be open to "hearing" me as a "helper" and not as a "critic."

I try to respect the purpose of the rehearsal and resist using it to compete with the director or prove my musicianship to him, and I very much appreciate a similar attitude from the director. I especially appreciate not being hastily criticized or accused in front of the choir.

As to the director's personal style of conducting, I have had the challenge of adapting to quite a few variations from director to director. To me, a good basic conducting technique includes a clearly defined vertical beat that can be easily understood by all those under direction. A clear downbeat that has a little bounce or rebound to it helps me to be more precise with the tempo and rhythm. When a director starts using both hands in a wide, horizontal, sweeping manner for expression, but neglects the underlying pulse, I have noticed that neither the choir nor I can be exactly sure where the beat is. The director who uses the right and left hands independently is much easier to follow.

I have sung and played for one director whose tempo was very clear, and his interpretation was very tasteful, but whose beat actually occurred at the top of his gesture, rather than at the bottom of it. For a long time, it seemed impossible for me to follow his directing until I got used to watching him for tempo and not for the specific beat. Because of the choir's overall ability and the clarity with which he directed the "and's," and not the "1's, 2's, 3's, and 4's," this was not as hard to discern as it could have been.

Another aspect of conducting technique which I appreciate in a director is giving attention to the accompaniment itself. (It is fortunate if the director is also a pianist, but it is not crucial.) It is so helpful when the director spends enough time with the music before rehearsal and knows it so well that he can conduct instrumental rhythm that might be different from the choral part. I am speaking primarily of passages in which the choir holds a chord for a number of beats while the piano or organ part has continuing rhythmic activity. Especially if there is a change of tempo in the accompaniment, I need to see the director's interpretation of it. Here again, the independent use of each hand is the key for me in following his communication.

In Performance

There is very little to be said about the relationship between director and accompanist with regard to the actual performance since hopefully most problems that would occur have been handled in rehearsal. However, if the performance is part of a worship service, and not a separate concert, then I, as accompanist, must be prepared for additional responsibility.

If there are hymns to be played, I appreciate knowing the preference of the director on the length of introductions and whether or not to begin the introduction while the director is announcing the hymn. In some informal services, I am asked to provide transition from one part of the service to the next, or from one hymn to the next. Sometimes there is to be a modulation on the final verse of a hymn. I like to know well in advance (like the choir rehearsal *before* the Sunday these things are required). Time spent before the service discussing these details helps me cooperate in keeping a smooth flow throughout the service.

Personality Blend

Finally, I have become aware that communication in a working relationship is deeply affected by the personalities involved. This may seem like an obvious statement, but too many times I have heard people say, "That's just the way I am," or "You've got to understand that I'm a little eccentric," and so on.

While there are some "ideal" matches among directors and accompanists, there are far more relationships that require conscious cultivation. And that cultivation almost always will improve the relationship, in spite of eccentricities or "the way we are." Cultivating the relationship with the accompanist will enhance the director's image as leader and the choir's confidence in his or her leadership as he or she and the accompanist work well together.

I appreciate a director who speaks affirmatively and courteously to me as well as to the choir. I can hardly tolerate open ridicule of myself or my musical abilities in the rehearsal room. If there is a problem that goes beyond routine musical criticism, the director should handle it privately outside of rehearsal time.

If it is true that we never really arrive as Christians or as musicians, but are in a constant state of growth and attempts to improve, then the perfect choral director does not exist. Neither, I might add, does the perfect accompanist. Since we are all involved in a growth process, I hope to work with a director who is striving to grow in his or her musical ability, spiritual commitment, and relationships with people. I feel I can do my best work with a director who encourages me and challenges me to be the best accompanist I can be for the Lord, for the overall choral program, and for my own growth and self-confidence as a man of God.

About the Contributor: *Owen Griffin has played for the Billy Graham Crusades since the fall of 1977 and writes most of the vocal arrangements for crusade soloists Tom and Terry Bledsoe. He holds a Master of Music degree, has taught theory as a graduate* *assistant and was a vocalist and keyboard player for New Hope, a concert touring ministry based in Thousand Oaks, California.*

In addition to playing in crusades, Owen was the accompanist, conductor and arranger for Suite Lady, a women's quartet which sang for churches, banquets, school assemblies and vocal backups for recordings. He is actively involved in the music program of First Baptist Church, Waco, Texas, and also enjoys travel, landscaping, gardening, and keeps physically fit with racquetball, swimming and other fitness activities.

Pat Terry

18.

What Teenagers Wish Choir Directors Knew

From the editor: *When I was fifteen years old, my friends and I thought that playing popular music on the hi-fi in someone's home at youth fellowship after church on Sunday night would be great fun—but we also knew it was out of the question because of the attitude of the adults in our church. But that was almost twenty years ago. And I realize that I feel no more in touch with teenagers today than I felt the adults at my home church were in touch with me back then.*

I think it is accepted that the teen years are a secretly serious time, yet one full of rapidly changing adventure, fun, pain, and joy. Finding out how to make contact, and communicate, and even minister to people in these years is often a confusing, frustrating task.

Pat Terry has sung hundreds of concerts, and teenagers respond to his haunting lyrics. They come down to talk to him after the concerts and pour out the feelings they've tried to express to other adults, but just couldn't find the words. Pat has put some of what he's learned in these pages, and perhaps it will shed some light for you about the teenagers in your own church.

I have spent the last nine years of my life doing concerts on campuses and in churches across the country. To say I've done some traveling would be an understatement. Now I realize that would hardly qualify me to be writing this chapter, but I have also spent much of that time listening to young people. What I have heard concerning music and Christianity has often disturbed me. I could not begin to count the times that I have been approached after a concert by some enthusiastic youthful listener and heard something like this:

"I really enjoyed the concert. I had never heard anything like it. The only Christian music I had ever heard was 'church music.' "

When the term "church music" was used, there was usually a drop in enthusiasm with an accompanying scowl that told me that the music to which they referred was probably close to the bottom of the list of their all-time favorite top ten. Not only have I heard these responses, but I have seen the church lose many promising young musicians to philosophies that eventually led them away into a musical expression that is no more than a propogation of humanism. These observations have caused me, and others who have a real desire for Christ to be glorified, to be grieved. The facts about the number of teenagers we are losing to secular music say something very negative to me about the way we communicate "our" gospel and what we are saying to the world around us about Jesus Christ. And although it is impossible to put the blame as to how this has happened on any one person or organization, it seems to me that, certainly, the church music minister could be a crucial agent in helping turn things around. He or she could make a vast difference in the overall outlook many teenagers have on music and how it can color one's outlook on life in general.

My conclusion is that if our Christianity is relevant, and I mean truly in tune with the needs of Christian people living in an anti-Christian world, then our music will and must be relevant too. Is that happening? Perhaps to some extent it is, but according to many of the youth I have spoken with, it is in some ways missing the mark. Much of what I will be saying in the next few pages will be my opinion drawn from my own experience and contact with teenagers. It is my hope that some of these observations will provide some food for thought and some insight into the needs of those to whom we are ministering.

The Search for Identity

One of the most important things that happened to me when I met Christ was that he established within me an identity of my own that needed no apology. It was based on the fact that

I was a child of God, certainly no better than anyone around me, but a unique part of God's family and that when all was said and done I was and am a winner. I could feel confident about my faith because of God's faithfulness.

Unfortunately it is often the case that the Christian young person struggles continually for a firm grasp on his or her identity. Psychologists tell us that the middle school and high school years in the life of the American teen are extremely tough in terms of establishing an identity. There is an incredible amount of peer pressure to be whatever is "in" at the time. Everything from haircuts to musical tastes can become standards according to which a young person is judged by his or her peers, and Christian and non-Christian alike feel the pressure. I think most Christian teens realize that their values are different from non-Christian teens, and their desire is to confidently live out those values, but they also have a need to somehow stay in touch and in tune with those around them. I guess the best way I can say it is that Christian teens don't mind being set apart for Christ; *they just can't stand being considered weird!* Read that a couple of times and don't forget it. It's one thing for the student to be labeled different because of his or her commitment to the Lord, but it's another to be labeled weird because his or her Christianity isn't big enough to apply to a secular surrounding.

Today's Christian young people seem to be in need of leaders who can help them not only develop a strong identity in Christ but also express it. It is a real struggle for many students to maintain a strong feeling of their identity in Christ and make it relevant to those around them. And it is often even more difficult because their churches don't seem to make a real effort to understand and assist in their struggles. If Tom, a young Christian, wants to be effective in reaching his friends for Christ, then he tries to live so that every area of his life says something about the completeness of God's love. If his grades are bad because of his own laziness, then Christ looks lazy, and if the music that Tom listens to and performs (as a choir member) is out-of-date and out of touch with his needs, then Christ looks out-of-date and insensitive.

I hope my point is becoming clear. To me, evangelism is not just the words that we say. Evangelism is the life we lead. If Christ doesn't make a difference in all that we are, then we can talk our heads off, and no one will care. Believe me, many young people who know Christ have told me that they are hungry for their lives to count for him. And they can often see right through religiosity and piety that lack content and concrete examples in the daily lives and attitudes of the adults in their churches.

Music is such a vital part of the American young person's identity and communication to his or her peers. The church music director can help to make the difference that sets the Christian apart more relevant to a young person's life. I realize that the music minister has pressures of his or her own. The more traditionally-minded members of the church could possibly frown upon some changes which might have to be made to make the church's music more relevant to teenagers. And there might even be times that the minister is labeled a radical. But I've had to ask myself, "Can we honestly be set apart for Christ and yet try to play it safe in the areas of music and communication?" Jesus himself was certainly a radical communicator and his total vision, a broad one and penetrating one, is what led to ultimate victory over sin and death. For the past two thousand years the world has not been able to forget about it either. Our goal then sounds clear enough . . . to help the young believer be confident in his or her identity in Christ and to help him or her express it. Can that be done in a musical format? I believe so, but to do it there are several areas that will need the immediate attention of those in leadership positions.

Recognizing the Barriers

An important first step is to admit that we adults have built some barriers through the years. The fact of the matter is that we have often been so concerned with keeping our music from being worldly that we have created music that only relates within our own comfortable "Christian" surroundings. It has become music for a subculture of people with certain expectations. Unfortunately the subculture has not had, in my opinion, a very balanced picture of what Jesus meant when he said, "I came that they might have life and might have it more abundantly." When we meet Christ, rather than losing our personality and revolving our whole life around a list of rules and regulations, I believe that on the contrary we are set free to be the persons that God always intended us to be. Within the authority of God's Word, we are free to experience and enjoy our lives without placing values on things according to whether or not they have the label "spiritual" on them. Being one of Christ's people is living in an attitude of thanksgiving for *all* of God's creation, and through our own creativity we give God the glory for his creative nature.

Now if we as Christians value music only because it can be used as some kind of musical tract or four-point sermon, then we have just built a barrier for the young person who wants to see Christ in every area of his or her life. He or she must start asking some questions. Questions like, "If music that talks directly about Christ is the only music that holds any real value, then what has Christ to do with all the other music that I hear?" And, "If he has no involvement with that, then does he care about my schoolwork, or my dating life or even a future vocation?"

It is probably tempting to think "Come on, Pat. Young people today don't think that way!" But resist that thought, because what they've told me shows they do. By approaching our music as Christians in such an exclusive manner, it seems to me that we have very subtly told the young person that there is a Christian world and a non-Christian world and Christ has very little if anything to do with the world outside of the church building. (By definition here, the Christian world is that atmosphere that I call devotional. It is our Bible study, our prayer life, our fellowship within the church, and even our terminology within the church.) These subtleties are, I believe, undermining true life in Christ and are making our evangelism sound hollow.

Now I am not saying that all of today's music is good. Much of it is communicating godless philosophies. But I really believe there is room for music that covers a variety of nonreligious subjects from a pure and godly viewpoint. It seems to me that the responsibility of the Christian who has been given a musical talent is certainly not to do away with all "Christian music" as we now know it. But in addition to the wonderful musical heritage we have received, I believe we should strive to help young people see that it's all right to sing a song about the wonder of a rainbow without mentioning a scriptural parallel, and still do it to the glory of God. They can do this because their singing and their attitude in doing it give testimony to the creativeness that God has given each of them. To say that a song like that would be unspiritual or unbecoming to a church choir is like saying that the Grand Canyon is unbecoming to God himself because it isn't in the shape of a cross.

I recently heard a well-known Bible teacher say that every time a lion roars he gives glory to the God that created him. Why? Because the lion has fulfilled a part of his uniqueness in

God's creation. It points to God and says, "Only God could have such unique variety in his world."

Now before you think that I have gotten a little too carried away on this theme, let me say that I realize that few people will fall on their knees in repentance simply because they hear a lion roar or because a church choir sings a song about rainbows or the Grand Canyon. But again, let me say that my reason for this observation is to show that we have had an unbalanced view of what music should be to believers. We have tried to spiritualize something that has no capacity for the spiritual. It seems to me that only people with spirits can be spiritual, not notes on a staff, and so it is when spiritual people present a well-rounded picture of life in Christ that music fulfills its purpose in our lives. Our music, in my opinion, should be a genuine comment on and reflection of the reality of Jesus Christ, alive and relevant to the world in which we live.

So I suggest that we can begin to break down the barriers we face by taking on and teaching an attitude of a well-rounded appreciation of music . . . all styles, from an intelligent scriptural viewpoint, with a variety of themes.

I think we need to look at another barrier that is perhaps a little more obvious than the one we just discussed. That is a language barrier. We Christians simply have a language all our own. We rarely "tell" anyone anything. We usually "share" it. We are frequently "blessed" and "burdened," "saved" and "sanctified" and even "filled" and "refilled." Those of us who know Christ are for the most part familiar with these terms, but quite honestly we have often confused many nonbelievers and cut ourselves off from many young believers by speaking such an exclusive language. There is certainly nothing wrong with any of these words within themselves but to try using them to relate your life style to a young non-believer or even a young or new Christian is like speaking Martian.

Several years back I visited the beautiful country of Germany and quickly found that when I did not at least make an effort to speak the German language, the nationals seemed to be offended. Their response was much like, "How dare that American! He tries to make us understand his language, but he has not even tried to speak our own." How true that often seems to me to be of much church music. It is just too foreign sounding to make sense to many young people and yet, as we have already discussed, they are hungry for some music that can help them see their faith as a reality in their everyday lives.

Language is not the only barrier that we face in our music today, however. Musical style is often a real hindrance to what we Christians are desiring to communicate through our music. Folk music was considered very contemporary in the church around 1965. I remember what a daring move it was when I was asked to bring my guitar to our church coffeehouse. But that was 1965, and now we have just moved into the '80s. The gospel has never changed and never will. It is a wonderful thing that God's Word is totally dependable and authoritative. But even though the gospel has not changed, musical styles and tastes have continually made changes throughout the years. So what is contemporary now?

Perhaps that is the question we should ask our youth groups. I recently overheard a young man at one of our concerts talking to his youth director. The youth director had made a statement that not many of the older members of the church were supporting the evening concerts, and the young man retorted, "We've been listening to their music for years. I think it's about time that they listened to some of ours!" Now it is a shame that there has to be a "theirs" and "ours" way of thinking within the church, but I guess we will have a difficult time ever getting away from the fact that different age groups usually have different musical tastes.

What the young man in the story was saying though is important. If we want to meet the needs of our young people, we are going to have to learn to listen to them. I am firmly convinced that if you ask your young people what is contemporary, they will tell you. Find out what vocal groups or solo singers both in secular music and in Christian music are the ones that are appealing to your youth, and make a point of finding out what makes that sound so appealing. Have a record party, do anything you have to in order to find it, but leave the confines of the rehearsal room and listen to some of today's music. You might even want to have some contemporary Christian music available for your youth choir to listen to, just to expose them to some new and different approaches to church music. They'll let you know right away what music is really making sense to them.

Though it's important to know what is currently popular and vital for the church, I think it's even more important not to be satisfied with simply emulating the latest sounds. The Christian has not set any new musical trends in who knows how long. You will probably have some ideas of your own, and by broadening your scope and exercising your own freedom there is little doubt in my mind that your young people will catch that enthusiasm and grow toward seeing their own potential.

The Battle within the Church

Since the earliest days of the church there has been a battle going on. It is a subtle one but one that makes a big difference in whether the church remains vital. Jesus himself faced this battle as he confronted the Pharisees of his day on the issue of their tradition as opposed to a vital relationship with a living God. How easy it is to fall into the same trap that these Pharisees were in. Here's an example.

The Scripture is very clear on the form of our church organization. It specifically gives us directives in the choosing of our elders and deacons and in their particular ministry functions. For us to be any less than obedient regarding these directions is to miss God's will because he has made it clear in his Word how they are to be handled. However, the Scripture is silent on some issues. For example, the Scripture never spells out what your order of worship should be for any given Sunday. But if we have ordered our services the same way for ten years, then it becomes easy to begin to "see" that order as an unchanging part of God's will. We almost treat it as if it *were* Scripture.

Now I believe that God's Word is always our authority, but where the Word is silent, then we have freedom under the guidance of the Holy Spirit. To me, it is not a good enough reason to do something simply because it has always been done that way before. According to the many conversations I have had, our young people are looking for a vitality that is not to be found when our local traditions become equal with our God.

Before I am misunderstood, allow me to say that there is certainly a place for tradition. I personally prefer a more traditional worship service, and I enjoy much traditional church music. But when I treat these traditions as being the authority when Scripture is silent, then I become the idolater—I have worshiped the creation and not the creator. If the church music minister desires to lead his or her young people in a vital musical direction, then I suggest he or she must hear the youths' cry for an honest vitality. It saddens me to hear so many young people say to me that they feel they are a part of a "dead" church when in reality the church is not dead, it has just been put to sleep by years and years of tradition. I don't really think these young people want to do away with what is good in the traditional areas of our worship and fellowship. They are just hungry to exercise the freedom to experience music that really communicates to them beyond the confines of their tradition.

The music minister faces quite a challenge here. He or she must try to lead and teach people who can sometimes be notorious for their unwillingness to learn—people in the congregation who strongly prefer to stay within traditional limits, or who are uneasy about more contemporary styles of music. Trying to do this will not be the easiest road to take, but I believe it is the one that will allow for growth and an openness for God to do new and exciting things within that minister's church. The subsequent results of such an approach can be exciting as well. In broadening our scope beyond what has worked in the past, we say to the world, and to each other and to ourselves, "Our God is a God of form and order in a world that has none, and he is a God of life, growth, change, and creativity within that perfect form."

Perhaps in looking back over my statements it seems hard to believe that any young person, especially those in your choir or youth group, ever really thinks in these terms. Well, no doubt they would probably say it differently, but in their questions and responses I have sensed many of the attitudes and perspectives that I have talked about.

It seems to me that it is only fair for us to step back and take an honest look at these matters. And it is my hope that after some thought and prayer you may find some of the ideas I have shared helpful to you in your ministry. I am convinced that your young people need you to take that honest look. But more than anything else that I have cited as a need in the lives of our youth today, I am certain that your young people need your love. They want you to accept them as they are and give them the chance to express themselves.

They want your advice (even when it seems that they don't), and they want you to love them enough to let them see your own struggles and mistakes. To reach our goal of ministering through a music that is truly relevant, I believe we can best do it through our honest love. Because whatever else may go wrong with our plans and programs . . . love never fails (1 Cor. 13: 8a).

About the Contributor:

Pat Terry is a Christian Communication song writer and minstrel. He has studied at West Georgia College, Antioch Bible Col-

lege, and has been a singer and songwriter for the last ten years. He traveled with the Pat Terry Group extensively across the United States, singing concerts on college campuses, in churches, and in concert halls. Now his concerts are solo, as he begins a new phase of his ministry.

Many of Pat's songs have been recorded by recording artists such as B. J. Thomas, Evie, Ray Price, Tom Netherton and others. Some of his songs are "Home Where I Belong," "I Can't Wait," "Nothing That You Can't Do," "Meet Me Here," and "All I Ever Need."

Pat and his wife, Pam, live in Smyrna, Georgia.

Katy Stokes

19.

What Choir Members Wish Choir Directors Knew

From the editor: *When was the last time you sat down with a choir member and had a really good talk? Sometimes, ministers of music have told me they feel set apart from the choir and the main congregation simply by the fact that they are on the staff. And as a choir member, I have often felt shy or reluctant to tell you how I really felt about what was going on. This chapter gives you a chance to read some things from a veteran choir member, whose easy way with words will thrill you, sober you, instruct you, warm you, and leave you feeling loved and needed.*

My father was the volunteer choir director of a small country church that on special days might have two hundred in worship. I was always intrigued with his sing-through choir practices where he let me sing along, feet swinging from an old wooden pew. Only on very unusual occasions would children and young people be allowed in the choir, so it was very exciting when he let me sing a duet with him one Sunday night. I was ten years old. Very accommodatingly he selected "Open My Eyes That I May See" because I could reach the C above middle C, the zenith of that choice song.

He probably suggested one day that I try the bottom note in the treble clef of the hymn book. I don't know for sure. Somewhere in the ebb and flow of adolescence I started singing alto. Somewhere, too, there was always a choir—and, of course, you, the choir director.

You come in all shapes and sizes, are usually terribly talented and strangely (a John Wesley "strangely") committed to music as a major vehicle of the soul in worship. In most of you there is a natural sensitivity to people who sing in your choirs. Of all mortals, you know what it is to sing with a group. But since society keeps changing, choir members probably do too, and perhaps there is a need to speak out on a few seemingly obvious traps a choir director can avoid.

After a search of three hours and nine minutes through the library stacks of *The Reader's Digest* from 1961 to 1967, I failed to find my favorite true story about a choir. So from memory and with due credit given, here is the anecdote anyway:

One summer morning as the choir in an eastern church was proceeding to its place in the loft, the tiny heel of a woman's pump (that explains the 1961–1967 time slot) caught in the vent of the floor furnace over which the choir marched. She simply slipped out of her shoe and not missing a note, limped on, leaving the shoe in the furnace grating. The obliging man behind her reached down as he passed to retrieve the shoe, swooping up, not only the shoe, but the grating as well. The unsuspecting bass following him promptly fell clattering into the furnace.

It all happened so quickly there was probably no way he could have avoided such a trap. Your hazards as a choir director are not as precipitous as the furnace was to the bass, but there are some things I, as a choir member of some thirty years, would like to talk about with you in my own serious, half-serious style. After all, we are good friends, and I appreciate you.

First of all, *know me* as a member of your choir. Here I am, a devoted church member, a good old girl who hasn't laid eternal and unaltering claim to a front and middle seat. I am not a professional singer, I *absolutely enjoy* singing in the choir. You can expect me to show up and learn the music in a respectable amount of time. Although I am one of the lesser lights, I don't want you to take me for granted, or worse yet, always make me be the one to share music, sit by the "brassy alto" all the time or move to the back row on Easter morning when the choir is fuller than usual.

Know who Charlie is, too. Even though he never appears to have a serious thought, croons a note or two and fairly swings through the responsive readings, he's often said that the *heartbeat* of the church of the living Lord for him is—the choir! He is not too involved in the committee structure of the church, nor does he attend a Sunday school class. Choir is where church is for him, and he is hoping you will get to know him well enough to see this. Besides, he is so much fun that the faces of the people sitting around him are always pleasant. He is outwardly irreverant, but deep inside, a delightful and committed person. *And* he has a great tenor voice.

Then there's Mary who is fairly emotional and, when moved by some facet of worship, has a little trouble singing. Your concerned reaction after her father's sudden death, when tears came unexpectedly and easily, was right on target!

The way you relate to your accompanist means a lot to me, too, especially when you lead me and my church to appreciate him or her. When the postlude is Vidor's "Toccata" or an arrangement of "Fill My Cup, Lord" at the conclusion of the service, I like to see you encourage the dispersing congregation to stand and listen by doing just that yourself.

Committed, emotional, irreverant, professional and nonprofessional, we are all sitting before you like an arrangement of variegated flowers in the budding stage. And since we're in the budding stage, I don't mind if you *push me* a little.

I really want to sing better, so a little vocal technique or a small lesson in voice placement or breathing can do wonders (even for that "brassy" alto). In rehearsals I really appreciate your warm-ups, vocalizing instead of leaping into next Sunday's anthem, and I've noticed that this prepares and preserves the voice for a better rehearsal.

Kurt Kaiser has done this with choirs I have sung in by having everyone hum a very gentle "ooo" on the same note. One section at a time, he works out a modulation so that the choir is taken from one key to another by half or whole step movement. He urges the choir to sing very softly so that our throats can relax and each one of us can start thinking of the total sound the choir is making.*

"It sets the frame of mind," Kurt claims, "and brings everybody together from the day's happenings."

When you *expect* us to improve in sound and sight reading, we will work to be better. I think there is potential in the smallest of choirs.

When I was eleven our pastor's wife, who later taught voice on the university level after her husband finished his seminary training, asked me to sing in a Christmas program what I thought was the strangest "song" I had ever heard. It was only the short

---

* Kurt Kaiser illustrates this warm-up in Chapter 9.

Recitative for Alto, "Behold! a virgin shall conceive" from *The Messiah.* In that small church and in those record-less, television-less, practically radio-less days, we had no knowledge of *The Messiah,* barely knew who Handel was. That amazing woman started where we were and pushed. Since then I have always waited expectantly for that particular recitative the many times our choir has sung the great oratorio. Bless Mrs. Miles!

On the other hand, it seems like a step backward when we altos, for instance, finally have a "decent solo part," to ask the sopranos to "help" us. Granted, you want to work for the very best sound you can get. But we want our chance to "shine."

"Push us, work with us, trust us!" any section may cry from time to time on the verge of making a giant step forward. So don't be afraid to push and *make definite preparation* for us. I remember that in the little church of my childhood, we had some fairly enthusiastic choirs, but no great choirs, probably because in rehearsal and in services we just "sang through" things. I have noticed one way to ease the pain of preparation is to get each choir member a folder in which to put pieces of music, perhaps even in the order of rehearsal.

Dr. Euell Porter, retired minister of music of Seventh and James Baptist Church in Waco, Texas and Professor of Choral Music at Baylor University, whom I consider to be a master of using rehearsal time, begins by saying something like, "Turn to page nine, circle E," and, starting at the *back* of a new piece of music, he works forward through the more difficult phrases. Then when we "take it from the top," there is a surprising sense of familiarity that breeds confidence. It is a little like walking your bike up a long hill so the ride from the crest can be more fun. Rather than starting at the beginning and bogging down, thinking "Whew! This is too hard for us," we feel like we are a super choir handling demanding music.

Preparation for *what* we sing is important to me, also. Of course, there are our favorite anthems. Our choir delights in Marshall's "My Eternal King." It is traditional and meaningful for the choir and the congregation, and we like to sing it a couple of times a year. On the other hand, I love very much to get new music. It is refreshing and helps keep me from feeling stale. And . . . it might surprise you to know that many people over fifty who, like me, have sung in your choirs are really eager to have a go at the Medema tempos and rhythms and all that other good "young music."

Preparation not only includes rehearsal plans and choice of music that *we* like, but conversation with the members of the church about what *they* would like to hear. Come to think of it, as you have probably noticed, congregations are seldom reluctant to tell you what they like and do not like—with varying degrees of tactfulness. Nevertheless, since all kinds of people are in the church, it makes sense to me to include all kinds of music.

When we work up some good music, I want you to flaunt it! Make a big thing of a musical event. The success of "Tell It Like It Is," "Celebrate Life" and that genre of Christian music have been due, not only to the singable songs, but the "Big Event" or production idea. My excitement builds, for example, when you actually set the date for a performance, announce it and start us working toward it. In fact, we can make *really big* plans when college students and other former choir members come home for holidays.

In my opinion, the theology of *gifts* is always appealing, and when you lead us to recognize that singing in the volunteer choir is using a gift God has given, it feels like the RSVP to an invitation. A church in Waco, Texas, makes a big thing of their RSVP Sunday when members of the church respond to the gifts God has given each person by participation in not only musical presentations, but displaying paintings, needlework, poetry, and eating food the culinary artists produce.

Every now and then I like for you to put the "gift-given" concept into words, perhaps something like this: "You people can sing. God gave you this gift. I think we need to use this gift for his glory in this choir in the best way we can." So, dear friend, *motivate me.*

When John Lindsey, now a teacher of violin at the University of Kentucky, was baptized, a member of his new church wrote, congratulating him on his commitment and action.

"When I consider your hours and hours of practice on the violin that were baptized also," the person wrote, "I am overwhelmed." John evidently felt the same way because as long as he was a member of that church, his violin solos soared to heaven as some magnificent incense from his gift on the altar in worship. Remind me that I, too, have a gift, small or large, that needs to be returned to God.

Another motivation for me is your emphasis on the message of the music we rehearse. If some biblical research is needed, I appreciate your digging into a commentary or two and giving me some background. This makes people and ideas come alive for me. Don't be afraid to intellectualize a bit—or dramatize. I'll eat it up!

The organist in my church is a deacon. It is impressive to me in worship when he slides off the organ bench and reads the scripture or leads the offertory prayer before slipping back to play Bach's "Arioso" or "Jesu, Joy of Man's Desiring." He is a part of the church, and his churchmanship says, "I'm serious in worship, too."

I love it when you can also be a part of the church, doing things like helping deliver in the Meals on Wheels program one day a week or teaching occasionally in the Adult Learning Center. I like to see you at fellowships. I like to feel you need us for something sometimes, just as we need you so much in your role as choir director.

I realize that you're busy, just as I am. In fact, I sometimes pant a little myself from the pace of life, committee meetings, vocational responsibilities as I come hurrying in to choir practice. So occasionally, *thank me* for my efforts. I do appreciate it if, when rehearsal needs to be longer than usual, you let me know ahead of time, if possible, so I can make any necessary arrangements with my family.

In a nutshell, I want you to know me, push me, prepare for me, motivate me and appreciate me. In turn, since I appreciate you, I hope you will pace yourself in your personal life as you do in your professional life. Yours is such a continuous responsibility, week in and week out in worship, that you have probably already discovered your need for re-fueling on a regular basis.

I have no idea what choir directors do to keep their spiritual and creative juices flowing. It probably runs the gamut from cooking, listening to records, going to a good movie, keeping a devotional time, watching a sunset or a sunrise to golf, tennis or jogging. Whatever, take care of the whole person. And remember, we love you.

About the Contributor: *Katy Stokes' career has been that of an Agathelian, a "creator of spiritual values, teacher of the young, developer of human abilities and harmonizer of personalities."* (Recovery of Family Life, *Elton Trueblood*). *She says, "I have found that the woman in the home is the 'continuing thread that holds the fabric of civilization together' * while freeing her*

(*Margaret Mead)

to take part in any number of creative activities," (such as singing in the choir.

Katy holds a B.A. degree from Baylor University and is the author of a column in Mabank Banner called "To The Stove and Back," and of a book, Paisano (The Story of a Cowboy and a Camp Meeting). *Katy has had more than fifty articles published in periodicals like "Youth in Action," "Church Recreation Magazine," "Baptist Student" and "Event."*

Katy also likes to square dance, birdwatch, play bridge and 42, read, entertain friends, cook, attend the symphony, entertain (or perform) with her husband, George, and sing in her church choir.

Index